T0160407

JANE BUTEL'S

QUICK & EASY SOUTHWESTERN COOKBOOK

ALSO BY JANE BUTEL

Jane Butel's Simply Southwestern

Jane Butel's Southwestern Kitchen

Jane Butel's Tex-Mex Cookbook

Jane Butel's Hotter Than Hell

Jane Butel's Finger Lickin' Rib Stickin' Great Tastin' Hot & Spicy Barbecue

Jane Butel's Freezer Cookbook

Fiesta

Chili Madness

JANE BUTEL'S
QUICK & EASY SOUTHWESTERN COOKBOOK

by Jane Butel

TURNER
PUBLISHING COMPANY

Turner Publishing Company
Nashville, Tennessee
New York, New York
www.turnerpublishing.com

Copyright © 2018, 1998 by Jane Butel

No part of this publication may be reproduced, stored in a retrieval system, or transmitted in any form or by any means, electronic, mechanical, photocopying, recording, scanning, or otherwise, except as permitted under Sections 107 or 108 of the 1976 United States Copyright Act, without either the prior written permission of the Publisher, or authorization through payment of the appropriate per-copy fee to the Copyright Clearance Center, 222 Rosewood Drive, Danvers, MA 01923, (978) 750-8400, fax (978) 750-4744. Requests to the Publisher for permission should be addressed to Turner Publishing Company, 4507 Charlotte Avenue, Suite 100, Nashville, Tennessee, 37209, (615) 255-2665, fax (615) 255-5081, E-mail: submissions@turnerpublishing.com.

Limit of Liability/Disclaimer of Warranty: While the publisher and the author have used their best efforts in preparing this book, they make no representations or warranties with respect to the accuracy or completeness of the contents of this book and specifically disclaim any implied warranties of merchantability or fitness for a particular purpose. No warranty may be created or extended by sales representatives or written sales materials. The advice and strategies contained herein may not be suitable for your situation. You should consult with a professional where appropriate. Neither the publisher nor the author shall be liable for any loss of profit or any other commercial damages, including but not limited to special, incidental, consequential, or other damages.

Cover design: Maddie Cothren
Book design: Mallory Collins

Library of Congress Cataloging-in-Publication Data

Names: Butel, Jane, author.
Title: Jane Butel's quick and easy Southwestern cookbook / by Jane Butel.
Other titles: Quick and easy Southwestern cookbook
Description: Nashville, Tennessee : Turner Publishing Company, 2018. |
  Includes index. |
Identifiers: LCCN 2017059432 (print) | LCCN 2017060438 (ebook) | ISBN
  9781681624754 (e-book) | ISBN 9781681624730 (pbk. : alk. paper)
Subjects: LCSH: Cooking, American--Southwestern style. | Quick and easy
  cooking.
Classification: LCC TX715.2.S69 (ebook) | LCC TX715.2.S69 B878 2018 (print) |
  DDC 641.5976--dc23
LC record available at https://lccn.loc.gov/2017059432

Printed in the United States of America
18 19 20 10 9 8 7 6 5 4 3 2 1

To all of my cooking school students and staff, who have been such a great inspiration. Their enthusiasm and helpful suggestions for my recipes were a wonderful asset in developing this book.

ACKNOWLEDGMENTS

I wish to thank all who helped me with the development of this book. First, to my editor, Shaye Areheart, who enthusiastically received the idea for the book and worked with me to get it in its final form. And to her always pleasant associate editor, Dina Siciliano, who was also very helpful.

My literary agent, Sidney Kramer, was a continual inspiration, assisting in completing all the necessary work to go to contract.

And to Trudy Fedora, MSRD, I wish to extend a heartfelt thanks for her meticulous analysis of the nutritional information for each recipe. She always went the extra mile, analyzing each recipe for the main as well as the optional ingredients, and it was such a delight and pleasure to work with her.

Contents

INTRODUCTION

This cookbook was written so that busy people who also want to be as healthy as possible can enjoy twenty-minute healthy recipes with the nutritional data annotated for each recipe. Cooking with chiles and other popular Southwestern ingredients is one of the best ways to maintain health.

I have had a lifelong love affair with the Southwestern "taste"—whether you call it Mexican, American Mexican, or Tex-Mex. Many of my happiest childhood memories are of the aromas of chile-laden dishes. I grew up in a food-loving family where both my mother and grandmother were graduate home economists, so the study of food was natural. And mastering Southwestern dishes was a must.

In our gardens we grew all types of chiles, garlic, herbs, robust tomatoes, and tons of corn, plus beans, squash, melons, and more.

My mother's favorite food was tamales. She was born in Corpus Christi, Texas, where she developed an early taste for them. Not the ordinary, run-of-the-mill variety, but really good homemade tamales. When I was a child, we always made them on the first cold Sunday afternoon in the fall and made enough for the entire holiday season.

Another strong influence on my young taste buds was my early introduction to authentic Mexican family cooking. For several years my uncle was in charge of a major American animal health program in Old Mexico. While there, he married a Mexican woman who had a culinary background.

During the years they lived in Mexico, we exchanged all kinds of recipes and food ideas. I learned the fabulous flavors of freshly made Mexican foods. Immediate favorites were homemade corn tortillas and flavorful refried beans, which my aunt looked down upon. (She thought we should eat much more sophisticated foods.)

Having grown up with a legacy of chile sauces and corn dishes, I have always felt that Southwestern foods are fun. The spicy flavors, bright colors, and contrasting textures make every meal a fiesta.

The tastes that are uniquely Southwestern have their roots in native populations, including Pueblo Indians, Aztecs, and Mayans. Working from a simple palette of ingredients, they honed the flavors through the centuries. Many of the results were brought about by necessity. Living in isolation, far from the ocean, shaped their culinary traditions.

The two pillars of the cuisine are chiles, which provide the personality, and corn, which provides a great deal of the structure. The chiles can be red, sun-ripened fruit or crisp and green. The corn is generally dried and soaked in lime (limestone) water to give it the characteristic taste. Fresh corn off the cob is also used.

Popular flavor accents are garlic, onion, cumin, Mexican oregano, and cilantro. There are, of course, others.

Whenever possible, keep a supply of fresh chiles and herbs in your refrigerator (or freeze them). The fresher, the better; stale, dried herbs and chile powders or pods do not taste as good as fresh.

With all of us leading ever busier lives, we sometimes compromise on our favorite flavors at mealtime because so many foods take too long to prepare. I wrote this book to show you many shortcuts and ways to take advantage of canned and frozen ingredients to create a much quicker and easier method of achieving the authentic flavors of Southwestern dishes. Every recipe in this book can be made in twenty minutes or less, and most recipes have five ingredients or fewer. Most of the recipes are very healthy too. You will find that each recipe has a nutritional analysis that details the calories, fat, sodium, and so on. I made every effort to cut the fats, sodium, and cholesterol. There are several recipes where just a few extra ingredients makes a special difference so I added those ingredients for flavor and called these recipes "Sunday Best."

For a complete collection of favorite American Mexican dishes, consult my Tex-Mex cookbook, also published by Harmony Books, a division of Crown Publishers, Inc., in 1980 and completely revised and edited and re-published in 2017 by Turner Publishing. Also consult my *Southwestern Kitchen*, which was published in 1994 and republished by Turner in 2016. This book was the basis for the PBS series *Jane Butel's Southwestern Kitchen*.

Before I decided to devote my career to writing and teaching about Southwestern cooking, I managed home economics and consumer marketing departments for General Electric, Con Edison, and Public Service Co. of New Mexico, then I developed a Consumer Affairs and Marketing Corporate Division for American Express. During this time I learned a great deal about efficient appliances and laborsaving tips that can trim hours from preparing everyday meals.

Following are some of my favorite laborsaving ideas:

- Get organized. A little time spent arranging your cooking gear can save lots of cooking time.
- Place items you use the most often in the handiest locations.
- Evaluate overall which is more important to you: saving time or money. In general, convenience and pre-prepped ingredients cost more. Examples are prepared salad greens, pre-shredded cheese, commercial stocks, and deli meats.
- Prepare ingredients for many dishes at the same time, such as chopping onions and mincing garlic. You can freeze chopped onion or garlic in frequently used amounts; it will keep for up to six months. Or place minced garlic in vegetable oil to cover in a jar in the refrigerator. It will keep for up to one month.
- Frequently used ingredients that require cooking and do not suffer when frozen can be cooked ahead and frozen in meal-sized quantities, ready for quick preparation. Examples are cooked pasta and rice and frequently used sauces, such as red or green chile sauce. Also, long-simmering stews can be made in quantity for quick meals later.
- When cooking, always read the recipe first. Then assemble the ingredients, making sure you have everything on hand or have a reasonable substitute.

- If cooked pasta or rice is called for and you have none on hand already cooked, boil the water while you are assembling the ingredients.
- Clean up as you go.
- Keep a 1-cup dry measure in frequently used food containers, such as flour, sugar, or oats containers.
- Get a good, accurate timer, such as a digital one, for timing quick cooking.

TIMESAVING COOKING AND FOOD PREPARATION TIPS

- Plan for time savings.
- When you have time, prepare frequently used ingredients, such as bread crumbs, in quantity.
- Prepare favorite spice combinations, such as rubs, in quantity.
- Make your own fresh herb salad dressing bases. Use them for salad dressings, bastes for meats, vegetable flavorings, and so on.

TIMESAVING EQUIPMENT

Get the best-quality equipment you can afford. Timesaving essentials are:

- *Microwave oven.* Can greatly speed up cooking most any Southwestern dish, particularly those that are stewed or steamed. Microwave ovens are not good for frying. Microwave energy is attracted to the most dense foods—fats, sugars, liquids, and bone. Cover the food so it cooks uniformly. Use a low power setting for defrosting and slower cooking.
- *Blender.* The best implement for pureeing and blending sauces. It is good for chopping small quantities but not for grating or shredding.
- *Food processor.* Performs many tasks a blender does but not as efficiently. Will shred, grate, and act as a small mixer, which a blender or a large electric mixer can't do.
- *Mini-chopper.* Not as essential as a blender or a food processor, yet a big time-saver for mincing garlic, chiles, and herbs.
- *Electric mixer.* Heavy-duty style, if used when baking.
- *Independent freezer.* If space allows.
- *Set of good-quality knives.* At least four or five knives.
- *Sharpening stone and steel.* For keeping knives sharp. (Sharp knives are quicker and safer to use than dull ones.)
- *Heavy, good-quality pots and pans.* At least for the basics: two 3-quart saucepans; two 10- to 12-inch heavy, seasoned skillets; and one or more 5-quart Dutch ovens.

LOW-FAT COOKING EQUIPMENT

To save calories—especially fat calories—and save time, be certain to have the following equipment on hand:

- *Heavy, nonstick seasoned skillet.* There are a number of good brands to select from. Choose one that has a nonstick finish that is also scratch resistant as opposed to a laminated nonstick finish. (These can delaminate with high-temperature pan broiling.)

- *Skillet grill.* Called a comal in the Southwest, it is handy for indoor grilling. There are also durable, heavy-gauge grills for indoor surface cooking.
- *Stovetop grills.* Handy and efficient for grilling indoors. Designed with a holding pan for the water and wood chips, they impart the taste of wood smoke.
- *Kitchen scales.* Excellent for weighing portions of foods such as pasta and individual servings of meats and such.
- *Measuring cups and spoons.* Critical for accurate measurement and good cooking results. For dry ingredient measuring, use a set of graduated measuring cups. For liquids, use clear glass or plastic ones with markings clearly designated on the side.
- *Fat separators.* Handy for defatting sauces and gravies.

Meal Planning

Use the basic food pyramid developed by the USDA and generally available to guide you in selecting a balanced diet with a good foundation of fresh fruits, vegetables, and grains.

- Set personal and family goals before you plan your menus for the week. Are there any specific objectives anyone has, such as weight reduction or fat reduction? By the way, fat is not a culprit in the *new* Southwestern cooking. Your goal should be to eat no more than 30 percent fat and no less than 15 percent. Each person's "fat budget" is about as personal as his or her bank account. An average woman (weighing 130 pounds) can have 47 grams of fat if fat is considered as 25 percent of her calories, of which there is a total daily calorie allowance of 1,700.
- Learn what fats are actually good for you, such as the fat in avocados and certain nuts (almonds, peanuts, and cashews). This monounsaturated fat is heart healthy.
- Look for as many whole grains as possible. Whole-wheat breads, tortillas (especially corn), pastas, bulgur, and couscous can be used alone or in combination with rice. Longer-cooking brown rice is especially nutritious and can be cooked ahead and successfully frozen.
- Legumes of all kinds are good for you. They come with the territory in this cuisine.
- Most any kind of bean is nutritious, especially pintos, the king of Southwestern beans. One cup has more than 50 percent of the fiber and folic acid needed to meet the U.S. recommended daily allowance (RDA). Pintos also have between 25 and 50 percent of the RDA of magnesium and iron and contain between 10 and 24 percent of the copper, zinc, and protein required daily.
- Eating meats and dairy products is a personal choice. Meats that are quick to prepare and the best for you are used in this book—cubed meats and boneless, skinless chicken or turkey breasts and cutlets or tenders. Cooked turkey and chicken breasts are convenient to have in frozen, ready-to-serve portions. Scallops and peeled ready-to-cook shrimp are quick; so are fish fillets and steaks and ground lean meat or turkey. And, of course, don't forget canned, water-packed tuna and canned clams for quick sauces.
- Fresh fruits and vegetables are healthy foods that are perfect in Southwestern cuisine. Scientists and dietitians agree that we should eat at least five servings a day. With the abundance of salsas, vegetable garnishes, and dishes containing lots of fruits and vegetables, you should not have a hard time including them in your diet. For convenience, frozen and canned vegetables can be used; they are harvested and preserved at the peak of goodness.

- For the greatest time savings, plan a week's worth of meals at once.
- Keep some quick-to-prepare entrées that you've made yourself in the freezer, space permitting.
- Plan to use seasonal foods. For example, root vegetables are in season in the winter and possess the needed vitamins and minerals for healthy winter nutrition. Fast roasting, as detailed in the recipe on page XXX, is a quick and delicious way to prepare root vegetables. Grilling is equally good.
- Preparing slow-cooked sauces and stews in quantity over the weekend or when you have extra time allows for effortless meals later.

The Southwestern cook has a well-balanced range of dishes to select from, including those that contain grains, vegetables, and meats. The addition of a simple salad and tortillas or bread makes a quick and delicious meal.

Basic Food Guide: Your Guide for Eating Well		
Food Group	**Suggested Daily Servings**	**Serving Size**
Bread, cereals, and other grain products; whole grain or enriched	6–11	1 slice bread; 1 ounce ready-to-eat cereal; 1/2 cup cooked cereal; 1/2 cup cooked pasta, rice, or grits
Fruits: oranges, melon, berries, apples, all other fruits	3–4	Whole piece of fruit; 1/2 cup juice; 1/4 melon; 1/2 grapefruit; 1/2 cup cooked or canned fruit; 1/4 cup dried fruit
Vegetables: dark green leafy, deep yellow starchy, all other vegetables	3–5	1/2 cup cooked or chopped raw vegetables; 1 cup leafy raw greens
Meat, poultry, fish, shellfish, egg whites, yolks (limit yolks to 4 per week), dried beans and peas, peanut butter	2 or 3 (Daily total of 6 ounces)	2–3 ounces cooked lean meat, fish, or poultry; 2 eggs; 4 egg whites; 1 cup cooked dried beans or peas; 2 Tablespoons peanut butter
Low-fat milk, cheese, yogurt	Calcium needs differ by age Children, teens, women up to age 25: 3 or 4 Women over 25 and men: 2 or 3	1 cup low-fat or skim milk; 1 cup low-fat yogurt; 1 1/2 ounces low-fat cheese
Fats: vegetable oils, salad dressings, spreads, nuts	Determine your fat allowance*	1 teaspoon butter, margarine, or mayonnaise; 1 Tablespoon salad dressing; 1 ounce nuts
Sweets, alcoholic beverages	Use common sense and consume in moderation	

*30 percent × 2,000 calories = 600 calories divided by 9 calories per gram of fat = 66.66 or 67 grams of total fat allowable per day.

Fat Reduction Tips

- Fat that you eat is easily converted to fat in your body. Two ways to eat less fat are to trim visible fat from meats and to chill stocks and skim the fat.
- Use less fat when you fry food. In fact, to pan-broil foods without using any oil or fat, use a well-seasoned, heavy skillet, preheating until medium hot. A good test to tell when it is hot is to sprinkle a bit of water on the surface, and when it dances, the skillet is hot. Exception: high-fat foods such as bacon should be started in a cold skillet to cook out most of the fat.
- In most recipes, one whole egg can be replaced with two egg whites. Or whole eggs can be replaced with a dehydrated egg substitute or an egg replacement product.
- Reduce the amount of oil in salad dressings, as I have in the recipes in this book.
- Reduce the amount of high-fat ingredients such as nuts and cheese.
- Substitute skim milk or buttermilk for whole milk. (Buttermilk sounds rich, but it is made from skim milk.) Substitute evaporated skim milk for cream—even heavy cream. The flavor will not be as rich, but the dish will have fewer calories and less fat.
- For cream cheese, substitute yogurt cheese, made by emptying a 16-ounce container of plain nonfat yogurt into a cheesecloth-lined strainer placed over a dish overnight in the refrigerator. Cheese will be made overnight and lasts about a week when kept covered. One 16-ounce carton yields about 8 ounces of cheese. You may also purchase light cream cheese or other light cheeses, including mozzarella and Monterey Jack, which is part mozzarella.
- Turkey is a good substitute for beef in many dishes. Ground turkey—especially turkey breast—has a fraction of the fat of ground chuck.
- Use less butter when eating bread and breakfast foods. Instead of butter for bread, try olive oil, which can be flavored with a bay leaf, herbs of your choice, and some crushed chiles or cracked pepper. Omit butter on pancakes, waffles, and breakfast breads.

Pantry Stocking Tips for a Southwestern Kitchen

Keep on hand a range of popular, ready-to-eat Southwestern food ingredients:

- Two or three different prepared salsas (canned, bottled, or frozen), such as a chipotle, a mild or medium tomato-based one for use in cooking, and a green salsa, plus others, as desired. When you have the time, you may want to prepare your own salsas and can or freeze them.
- Low-sodium, low-fat canned chicken, vegetable, and beef broth. When homemade, it's called stock.
- Canned or frozen green chiles
- Ground and crushed red chiles, especially ground mild and hot chiles and crushed northern New Mexican caribe and hotter pequin chiles
- Pickled jalapeño chile slices
- Condiments, such as black olives
- Canned or cooked and frozen pinto and black beans
- Vinegars, especially cider, white, red wine, and balsamic
- Prepared jalapeño jam and/or jelly

- Tortillas. All kinds, whether they are corn or wheat, bought or homemade, freeze well.
- Chile-laden sauces, such as red chile enchilada sauce or adobo sauce. They can be frozen almost indefinitely. Although they are not particularly time-consuming to make, it is convenient to have several meal-sized quantities frozen and ready for use.

BASIC PREPARATIONS

- *Green chile:* To parch green chiles, rinse them first, leaving the stem on, then place on either a foil-lined baking sheet or a broiler pan and pierce close to the stem with a sharp knife to prevent bursting. For electric broilers, place the top of the chiles 3 to 4 inches away from the broiler unit; rotate them as they brown and blister. For gas broilers, place the chiles' surface about 1 to 2 inches under the broiler or place them on top of an outdoor grill. When uniformly blistered, plunge them in ice water. Drain and peel if using immediately. Or to store for later use freeze them on a cookie sheet separating them so they do not freeze together and freeze until firm, then place in freezer-weight plastic bags.
- *Cilantro*: Whenever using fresh cilantro in a salsa, guacamole, or any relish where it is served raw, always coarsely chop it. Mincing it creates a strong, disagreeable odor and flavor.

*A "Sunday Best" recipe with more than five ingredients but fewer than ten.

APPETIZERS

Southwestern appetizers always set a fiesta mood. The clear, bright, spicy flavors overlaid with the tart, tangy taste of lime and other fruits complemented by various corn, vegetable, and cheese combinations wake up even the most tired palate.

This collection of appetizers includes quick and easy dishes that are not as heavy as traditional appetizers, which are made with lots of cheeses and fried tortillas.

With Southwestern appetizers, margaritas are a standby and are frankly hard to beat. Other excellent choices are complementary wines, of which there are many. When in doubt, I choose champagne. Beer has long been a popular accompaniment to Mexican food. The first beer production on the American continent was in Mexico and was started by German immigrants.

Of course, nonalcoholic flavored waters, fruit juice combinations, nonalcoholic wines, and iced teas are all thirst quenching.

Scottsdale Toasts with Chile Jack Melt

Known as bruschetta in Italy, these snacks or light meals can be made ahead or served buffet style. This allows guests to prepare their own with the toppings they like. To melt the cheese, have a toaster oven or grill handy (if the grill is hot for the rest of the meal) and let your guests fix their toasts to order.

COOKING TIME: 2 to 3 minutes
YIELD: 4 to 8 servings

     8 thick slices crusty bread, toasted, or 8 (4-inch) flour tortillas
   1/2 cup fresh tomato-based salsa or Salsa Fresca (recipe on page 159)
     1 cup coarsely shredded Monterey Jack, Cheddar, or combination, or goat cheese

If you are using tortillas, heat them in a plastic bag in the microwave oven at full power for 20 seconds each (1 1/2 minutes for eight), or wrapped in aluminum foil in a 350°F (180°C) oven for about 10 minutes, or on a grill for 3 to 5 minutes, or individually over a burner for a few seconds per side.

Spread each toast or tortilla with 1 Tablespoon of the salsa, and sprinkle with some of the cheese. Place under the broiler or on the grill for about a minute or until the cheese melts. Serve hot.

VARIATIONS: Other toppings include coarsely chopped cooked meat such as chorizo sausage or chilied beef, shredded chicken, drained black or pinto beans, or any grilled vegetable.

PER SERVING (1/8 recipe): Calories 178, Protein 8 g, Carbohydrates 23 g, Fiber 1 g, Fat 6 g, Saturated Fat 3 g, Cholesterol 13 mg, Sodium 339 mg

Guacamole

This is probably the most popular Southwestern appetizer after tostados and salsa. Perfect guacamole results when you dice the avocados into 1/2- to 3/4-inch squares, then carefully add all the other ingredients in the order listed, stirring minimally. For the best flavor, always use fresh ingredients.

PREPARATION TIME: 10 to 12 minutes
YIELD: 4 servings

      2 Hass avocados, soft when pressed with thumb
   1/2 lime
   1/4 cup chopped fresh tomato
      1 clove garlic, minced
   1/4 cup chopped onion
      1 fresh jalapeño chile, minced
   1/2 teaspoon salt or to taste, optional
      3 Tablespoons coarsely chopped cilantro, optional

Slice the avocados in half and scoop out the flesh. Cut into 1/2-inch dice, using two knives. Place in a medium bowl. Squeeze some of the lime juice over the avocado. Add most of the tomato, garlic, onion, and jalapeño, reserving some if the avocados are small. Fold in carefully so as not to mash the avocado. Taste and add the salt, if desired. Add the rest of the lime juice, tomato, onion, jalapeño, and cilantro (if using), if needed for flavor. Serve in an earthenware bowl with tostados or corn chips or fresh vegetable crudités.

PER SERVING: Calories 173, Protein 2 g, Carbohydrates 10 g, Fiber 5 g, Fat 16 g, Saturated Fat 2 g, Cholesterol 0 mg, Sodium 12 mg

Pinto Pate

A close kin to refried beans but lighter and more highly flavored for smearing on crisp Tortilla Toasts.

COOKING TIME: 5 to 6 minutes
YIELD: 4 to 8 servings

1	teaspoon extra-virgin olive oil, preferably Spanish
1/4	cup coarsely chopped onion
2	cloves garlic, coarsely chopped
2	cups cooked pinto beans or 1 (15-ounce) can, drained
1/2	cup chopped green chiles (2 fresh chiles, parched [instructions on page xvii] and peeled, or frozen or canned chiles)

Heat the oil in a saucepan or skillet. Add the onion and garlic and sauté until they become clear and slightly browned. Place the onion mixture, beans, and chiles in a food processor or blender and process until coarsely chopped or mash with a potato masher while in the skillet. Return to the pan and heat until warm. Serve with Tortilla Toasts (recipe on page 6) or use as a layer on Southwestern Pizzas (recipe on pages 52–55).

PER SERVING (1/8 recipe): Calories 70, Protein 4 g, Carbohydrates 13 g, Fiber 4 g, Fat 1 g, Saturated Fat 0 g, Cholesterol 0 mg, Sodium 316 mg

Blue Corn Tortilla Toasts
with Salsa Marinated Mexican "Caviar"

Using blue corn tortillas for canapes makes these toasts a real Southwestern flavor treat. White or yellow corn tortillas can be substituted.

PREPARATION TIME: 10 minutes
YIELD: 4 to 8 servings

  8 blue corn or other corn tortillas
  1 cup well-drained garbanzos (sometimes called chickpeas)
1/2 cup salsa, any type
1/2 lime, juiced
  2 Tablespoons coarsely chopped cilantro

Preheat the oven to 425°F (220°C). Prepare the tortillas as on page 6. Meanwhile, prepare the "caviar" by combining the garbanzos with the salsa and lime juice in a bowl. Taste and adjust the seasonings. Stir in most of the cilantro, reserving some for garnish. Serve in a bowl on a platter with the Tortilla Toasts (recipe on page 6) encircling the bowl. Top the "caviar" with the reserved cilantro.

Note: Any leftover garbanzos can be used in salads or in rice dishes or combined with vegetable medley dishes.

PER SERVING (1/8 recipe): Calories 95, Protein 4 g, Carbohydrates 19 g, Fiber 3 g. Fat 1 g, Saturated Fat 0 g, Cholesterol 0 mg, Sodium 134 mg

Tortilla Toasts (Baked Tortilla Chips)

Baking tortillas avoids frying them in fat, although it makes them a bit tougher and some say less flavorful. But sprinkling the tortillas with water before baking and seasoning them enhances the flavor so you hardly miss the fat.

You can bake corn or flour tortillas. Different seasonings vary the flavor.

PREPARATION TIME: 10 minutes
YIELD: 6 or more servings

12 (6- to 8-inch) corn or wheat-flour tortillas
Seasoning of your choice, such as Southwestern seasoning salt or rub, ground pure red or green chile, dry Southwestern salad dressing, freshly squeezed lime juice, ground cumin, or dip mix

Preheat the oven to 425°F (220°C). Place the tortillas on a cutting board and cut them into 4 to 6 pieces. Arrange evenly on one large or two medium baking sheets.

Dip your fingertips into a small bowl of water and sprinkle the tortillas, or spray with a mister. Place the tortillas in the oven and bake for 5 minutes. Turn each piece and bake for 5 minutes longer. Remove from the oven and lightly sprinkle with whatever seasoning you wish, or shake the pieces in a bag containing the seasoning. These chips are best served warm. Freeze any remaining for reheating and serving later.

PER SERVING (1/6 recipe or 2 corn tortillas): Calories 115, Protein 3 g, Carbohydrates 24 g, Fiber 3 g, Fat 1 g, Saturated Fat 0 g, Cholesterol 0 mg, Sodium 84 mg (Analyzed without seasonings.)

Nacho Crisps with Goat Cheese, Fruit, and Lime Salsa

The savory flavor of the goat cheese complements the tart fruit-lime salsa. You can substitute whatever fruit is in season, if you prefer. This is a "Sunday Best" recipe.

PREPARATION TIME: 10 to 12 minutes
YIELD: 4 servings

      8 corn tortillas
      1 cup chopped fresh nectarines, peaches, pears, or any firm-fleshed fruit
      2 scallions, including the tender green tops, minced
      2 cloves garlic, minced
   1/4 cup freshly squeezed lime juice (1 large or 2 small limes)
      4 ounces goat cheese or cream cheese

Preheat the oven to 425°F (220°C). Stack the tortillas on a cutting board and cut into quarters. Arrange evenly on one large or two medium baking sheets. Bake for 5 minutes. Turn each piece and bake for another 5 minutes or until crisp.

Meanwhile, prepare the salsa by combining the fruit, scallions, garlic, and lime juice in a bowl. Remove the crisps from the oven and let cool. Spread each with the goat cheese and top with the salsa. Or serve the cheese and salsa in separate bowls and arrange the tortilla crisps around the edges so each person can spread their own.

PER SERVING: Calories 217, Protein 9 g, Carbohydrates 31 g, Fiber 4 g, Fat 7 g, Saturated Fat 4 g, Cholesterol 13 mg, Sodium 189 mg (Analyzed with nectarines.)

Calabacita Crisps

Squash have always been abundant in the Southwest. In fact, calabacitas are the original wild squash. Nowadays *calabacita*, the Spanish word for squash, is used for any type of squash. These crisps offer a flavorful alternative to tostados or tortilla chips for dipping.

COOKING TIME: 15 minutes
YIELD: 4 servings

    4 medium zucchini or yellow summer squash
    1 egg white
 3/4 cup cornflake or tortilla chip crumbs, finely ground
    2 Tablespoons ground pure mild or hot red chile, depending on desired spiciness
    2 cloves garlic, finely minced

Preheat the oven to 425°F (220°C). Cut the squash lengthwise into 1/4-inch slices. Place the egg white in a liquid measuring cup and beat well with a fork, then add water to measure 2/3 cup. In a shallow bowl or pie plate, combine the crumbs, chile, and garlic; mix well.

Dip the squash slices into the egg white mixture, then into the spiced crumbs. Place on a baking sheet and bake for about 15 minutes, or until crisp and golden. Serve warm with a salsa or as is for a light snack.

PER SERVING: Calories 128, Protein 5 g, Carbohydrates 27 g, Fiber 5 g, Fat 1 g, Saturated Fat 0 g, Cholesterol 0 mg, Sodium 252 mg (Analyzed with cornflake crumbs.)

Spicy Bacon Bites

A rather unlikely appetizer, but very tasty, especially before a brunch.

COOKING TIME: about 10 minutes
YIELD: 4 to 6 servings

- 1 large egg or 2 egg whites, beaten
- 1 Tablespoon ground pure hot red chile or to taste
- 1 teaspoon Dijon mustard
- 1 cup finely ground toasted, fresh bread crumbs
- 6 slices thickly cut bacon, cut into 2-inch pieces

Preheat the oven to 375°F (190°C). Place the egg in a shallow pie plate and add 2 Tablespoons water, the chile powder, and mustard; mix well. Place the crumbs on a paper plate.

Set a baking sheet next to the crumbs. Dip each piece of bacon into the egg mixture, then the crumbs; place on the baking sheet. Bake until golden and crisp, about 10 minutes. Drain and serve warm.

PER SERVING (1/6 recipe): Calories 139, Protein 6 g, Carbohydrates 14 g, Fiber 1 g, Fat 6 g, Saturated Fat 3 g, Cholesterol 45 mg, Sodium 439 mg

Chile Cheesed Tortilla Roll-Ups

These pinwheels are easy to make and popular in the Southwest. You can vary the ingredients widely, using any good melting cheese and any favorite chiles.

COOKING TIME: 2 minutes in a microwave oven, 10 minutes in a conventional oven
YIELD: 6 to 8 servings

    4 (10-inch) white-flour tortillas
1 1/2 cups shredded Cheddar cheese or mixed Cheddar and Monterey Jack cheeses
  1/4 cup minced pickled jalapeño chiles
    2 Tablespoons crushed caribe red chile
    1 cup salsa or combination of lettuces

If using a conventional oven, preheat to 425°F (220°C). Lay the tortillas on a flat surface and sprinkle with the cheese. Scatter with the jalapeños and chile.

Roll each tortilla and secure with a skewer or toothpick. Place on a baking sheet (for a conventional oven) or on a plate (for a microwave oven). Cover the baking sheet with aluminum foil, place in the oven, and bake for 10 minutes, or until the cheese is melted. (Or place the plate, uncovered, in the microwave oven for about 2 minutes at full power for all 4 rolls.) Cut the roll-ups diagonally into 1/4-inch-thick slices. Serve warm on a bed of salsa or lettuce.

PER SERVING (1/8 recipe): Calories 213, Protein 9 g, Carbohydrates 22 g, Fiber 2 g, Fat 10 g, Saturated Fat 5 g, Cholesterol 22 mg, Sodium 320 mg (Analyzed with Cheddar cheese.)
PER SERVING (1/8 recipe): Calories 164, Fat 4 g, Saturated Fat 1 g, Cholesterol 4 mg (Analyzed with low-fat Cheddar cheese.)

Black Bean and Goat Cheese Chalupitas

This combination of flavors is a sure winner. The tostados, black beans, and goat cheese can be prepared ahead for last-minute assembly.

COOKING TIME: 3 to 5 minutes
YIELD: 4 to 6 servings

24 tostados, bought or homemade (recipe on page 6)
 1 (16-ounce) can refried black beans
 4 ounces (1/2 cup) goat cheese, preferably with Southwestern flavorings added*

Preheat the broiler. Place the tostados on a baking sheet. Spread each with a layer of black beans, then the cheese. Place under the broiler for 3 to 5 minutes, until lightly bubbled. Serve hot.

* To prepare the Southwestern-flavored goat cheese if it is not commercially available, add to the cheese 1 teaspoon ground pure mild red chile, 1 clove garlic, minced, and a pinch of cumin; stir to blend. Cream cheese can be substituted for the goat cheese.

Note: Any leftover black beans can be placed in a moisture-proof bag and frozen for up to 90 days.

PER SERVING (1/6 recipe): Calories 190, Protein 9 g, Carbohydrates 24 g, Fiber 5 g, Fat 6 g, Saturated Fat 3 g, Cholesterol 9 mg, Sodium 336 mg

Shrimp de Ajo with Refried Black Beans

These are a "gussied up" version of nachos. The Caribbean or southern Mexican influence is felt here with the black beans and shrimp. A lime-edged salsa brings out and complements the flavors. This is a "Sunday Best" recipe.

COOKING TIME: 5 minutes
YIELD: 4 to 6 servings

      4 cloves garlic, minced
   1/4 cup freshly squeezed lime juice (1 large or 2 small limes)
     24 medium, uncooked shrimp, peeled and deveined
       1 (16-ounce) can refried black beans
     24 baked tostados, bought or homemade (recipe on page 6)
 1 1/2 cups lime-based salsa (recipe on page 161), or commercial salsa with the juice of 1 lime added

Preheat the broiler to low. In a large bowl combine the garlic and lime juice; stir in the shrimp. Place the tostados in a single layer on a baking sheet. Spread a spoonful of the beans on each tostado, then top with a shrimp. Place under the broiler for about 5 minutes, or until the shrimp are pink and tender; do not overcook. Serve with the salsa.

PER SERVING (1/6 recipe): Calories 190, Protein 11 g, Carbohydrates 30 g, Fiber 6 g, Fat 3 g, Saturated Fat 0 g, Cholesterol 37 mg, Sodium 360 mg

Grilled Veggie Bites with Spicy Salsa

Most any kind of grilled vegetables are wonderful served many ways. They make a good snack to munch on as the rest of the meal grills.

COOKING TIME: 14 minutes
YIELD: 4 servings

2 (5- to 6-inch-long) zucchini, rinsed and sliced lengthwise into 1/4-inch-thick slices
1 large or 2 small red onions, sliced crosswise in 1-inch-thick slices
1 Tablespoon crushed caribe red chile flakes
1 cup any spicy salsa such as Hot New Mexican Table Salsa (recipe on page 158)

Place the zucchini and onions on a baking sheet. Sprinkle the chile flakes on both sides. Meanwhile, heat the grill to medium-high, placing the rack about 3 inches from the coals or flame.

When the fire is hot, grill the onions for about 10 minutes or until soft. Turn, add the zucchini, placing directly on the grill or in a mesh screen holder for about 2 minutes, then turn again and grill on the other side. The vegetables should be almost fork-tender and browned in places. Cut the zucchini into 1-inch-wide strips. Serve the zucchini and onions with a bowl of toothpicks and a bowl of the salsa.

PER SERVING: Calories 55, Protein 3 g, Carbohydrates 12 g, Fiber 4 g, Fat 1 g, Saturated Fat 0 g, Cholesterol 0 mg, Sodium 75 mg

Fire Powered Popcorn

Mix your own rub or purchase a chile-based rub (see the online order sources on page 209).

COOKING TIME: 3 to 5 minutes
YIELD: 2 to 4 servings

2/3 cup popcorn kernels
3 Tablespoons vegetable oil (omit if popping in an air popper)
1 teaspoon Basic Rub (recipe on page 173) or purchased dry rub

Pop the corn with the oil (if using), following the manufacturer's instructions. Place the rub in a bag or mixing bowl. Mix the popcorn with the rub, shaking the bag or stirring the bowl. Serve warm.

PER SERVING (1/4 recipe): Calories 128, Protein 4 g, Carbohydrates 25 g, Fiber 5 g, Fat 2 g, Saturated Fat 0 g, Cholesterol 0 mg, Sodium 167 mg (Analyzed without oil for popping.)

Hot Chile Almonds

These are marvelous for snacks. You can use any favorite nut, from peanuts to pistachios. This is a "Sunday Best" recipe.

COOKING TIME: 20 minutes
YIELD: 2 cups

1	teaspoon extra-virgin olive oil, preferably Spanish
2	Tablespoons ground pure red hot chile
1/2	teaspoon ground cumin
1/2	teaspoon garlic granules
1/2	teaspoon coarse salt
2	cups whole almonds

Preheat the oven to 300°F (150°C). In a medium bowl mix the oil with the chile, cumin, garlic, and salt. Add the nuts and stir to coat. Place in a single layer on a baking sheet. Bake for 15 minutes. Stir and bake for 5 or more minutes or until toasted. Serve warm or seal until ready to serve.

PER SERVING (1/4 cup): Calories 225, Protein 8 g, Carbohydrates 8 g, Fiber 5 g, Fat 19 g, Saturated Fat 1 g, Cholesterol 0 mg, Sodium 165 mg

Quesadillas

Quesadillas are one of the most versatile of all light meals or appetizers. Literally translated, *quesadilla* means "cheese detail." Restaurants in Old Mexico serve a much simpler version of quesadillas. There, generally, a quesadilla is a freshly baked corn tortilla oozing with quick-melting cheese and served with a side dish of freshly made salsa. Sometimes they are fried, though often not. However, quesadillas have benefited from enormous innovations in Southwestern cooking in the United States in the past few years. You can find quesadillas made with all kinds of fillings—any kind of cheese paired with meats, seafood, stewed or seared vegetables, and a vast assortment of salsas. Dessert quesadillas are even possible.

Quesadillas are one of the most fun foods to garnish and present in creative and pretty ways. Just use your favorite or on-hand ingredients and let your imagination roll. In our cooking schools we are constantly surprised by how many ways our students prepare beautiful and flavorful quesadillas. Don't forget salsas, squirt bottles, and confetti tosses of chiles and minced parsley.

The three constants for American quesadillas are wheat-flour tortillas, quick-melting cheese, and pickled jalapeños.

COOKING TIME: 2 to 3 minutes
YIELD: 1 quesadilla

1	teaspoon unsalted butter, melted
1	(10- to 12-inch) wheat-flour tortilla
2 to 4	Tablespoons shredded Monterey Jack and Cheddar cheese combination or any substitution, such as goat cheese, Muenster, Asadero, or other quick-melting cheese
6 to 8	slices pickled jalapeño chiles
	Other fillings as desired: sautéed chorizo, sliced grilled chicken, baby shrimp, cooked pinto or black beans, chilied meats, any sliced seared vegetables, chopped onion, and tomato

Preheat a comal (cast iron griddle), tapa, or griddle to medium heat. Brush some of the butter lightly in the shape of half a tortilla on one side of the comal. Place the tortilla on the butter. Place the cheese on the buttered half of the tortilla, allowing a 1/2-inch margin around the edge of the tortilla. Scatter the jalapeño slices and any other fillings over the cheese.

When the cheese starts to melt, fold the other half of the tortilla over the fillings and lightly press until the edges hold together. Brush the top with more of the butter. Flip the quesadilla by gently placing a pancake turner under the curved edges of the quesadilla and rolling it over. Cook until browned. Remove from the heat, slice into 4 or more sections, and garnish as desired. Serve warm.

PER SERVING: Calories 326, Protein 10 g, Carbohydrates 41 g, Fiber 2 g, Fat 13 g, Saturated Fat 6 g, Cholesterol 24 mg, Sodium 510 mg

Quickie Quesos

Simple, good so many ways, and such a quick snack or appetizer.

COOKING TIME: 8 to 10 minutes
YIELD: 6 servings

  6 **corn tortillas**
  1 **cup coarsely shredded Cheddar and Monterey Jack cheeses**
1/4 **cup coarsely crushed caribe chile**
  3 **green chiles, peeled and chopped, or 1 (4-ounce) can chopped green chiles**

Preheat the oven to 425°F (220°C). Arrange the tortillas on a baking sheet. Place in the oven and bake for 6 to 8 minutes, until slightly crisp. Remove from the oven and sprinkle evenly with the cheese.

Return to the oven and bake for 2 to 3 minutes more, until the cheese is melted. Remove from the oven and sprinkle with the caribe and green chiles. Cut each tortilla on a cutting board into 4 pieces and arrange as desired on a warm platter. (Warm the platter while the cheese is melting.) Serve warm.

VARIATIONS: Olives, chilied meat, or most any pizza topping can be used to top these tortillas. Salsas are great for dunking.

PER SERVING: Calories 154, Protein 7 g, Carbohydrates 17 g, Fiber 3 g, Fat 8 g, Saturated Fat 4 g, Cholesterol 18 mg, Sodium 203 mg

Stuffed Jalapeño Chiles

These are so good when you prepare them yourself. They are much better than store-bought. And so easy. A good friend of mine, Sam Arnold, who is no longer with us, served these stuffed with peanut butter in his Fort Restaurant in Denver.

PREPARATION TIME: 15 minutes
YIELD: 6 servings

18 whole pickled jalapeño chiles
1/4 cup peanut butter, preferably crunchy
1/4 cup spicy Southwestern-flavored goat cheese (see page 11)
6 large cooked, peeled, and deveined shrimp

Slit each jalapeño lengthwise. Remove the seeds and blot out excess juice. Stuff 6 jalapeños with the peanut butter, 6 with the cheese, and 6 with the shrimp. Serve on an attractive platter as finger food.

PER SERVING (1 jalapeño): Calories 67, Protein 3 g, Carbohydrates 3 g, Fiber 1 g, Fat 5 g, Saturated Fat 1 g, Cholesterol 0 mg, Sodium 112 mg (Analyzed with peanut butter.)
PER SERVING (1 jalapeño): Calories 31, Protein 2 g, Carbohydrates 1 g, Fiber 0 g, Fat 2 g, Saturated Fat 2 g, Cholesterol 5 mg, Sodium 98 mg (Analyzed with goat cheese.)
PER SERVING (1 jalapeño): Calories 9, Protein 1 g, Carbohydrates 1 g, Fiber 0 g, Fat 0 g, Saturated Fat 0 g, Cholesterol 11 mg, Sodium 73 mg (Analyzed with shrimp.)

Double Corned Fritters with
Quick-Smoked Shrimp and Jalapeño Lime Creme Dressing

These corn fritters are quick to make from grilled corn and are delicious served warm with Quick Smoked Shrimp (recipe follows) and Jalapeño Lime Creme Dressing (recipe on page 48). This is a "Sunday Best" recipe; however, the fritter batter can be made ahead for last-minute serving.

COOKING TIME: 1 minute each
YIELD: 4 to 6 servings (12 to 18 fritters)

2	ears yellow corn, grilled (can be leftover)
1	large egg
1 1/4	cups buttermilk
1	Tablespoon vegetable oil
1/2	cup chopped green chile
1/2	cup yellow or blue cornmeal or corn flour
1/2	cup all-purpose flour
1/2	teaspoon baking soda
1	teaspoon baking powder
3/4	teaspoon salt
16	Quick-Smoked Shrimp (recipe follows) or Guaymas Shrimp (recipe on page 79)
	Jalapeño Lime Creme Dressing (recipe on page 48)

Cut the corn off the cob. In a bowl add the egg, buttermilk, oil, and chile and mix well. In a separate bowl combine the cornmeal, flour, baking soda, baking powder, and salt. Add to the buttermilk mixture. Stir just until blended, then stir in the corn.

Preheat a griddle. Ladle enough batter onto the griddle to make 12 to 18, 2-inch pancakes. Arrange 3 per serving in a somewhat vertical overlapping stack with the shrimp. Serve with the Jalapeño Lime Creme Dressing or a salsa of your choice and sour cream.

To Quick-Smoke Shrimp

Preheat the oven to 425°F (220°C). Rinse the shrimp and season with salt and black pepper and a squeeze of lime. In the bottom of a heavy pot with a close-fitting cover that will not be damaged by smoke, place black tea leaves or contents of 1 tea bag. Place a metal trivet in the bottom of the pot and arrange the shrimp on it. Place the lid on the pot and set it on a surface unit or burner on medium-high heat for about 5 minutes, or until smoke starts to emerge from under the lid. Then move the pot to the oven for 5 minutes.

PER SERVING (1/6 recipe): Calories 216, Protein 12 g, Carbohydrates 31 g, Fiber 2 g, Fat 5 g, Saturated Fat 1 g, Cholesterol 65 mg, Sodium 610 mg

*A "Sunday Best" recipe with more than five ingredients but fewer than ten.

Pronto Beef, Pork, Veal, and Lamb

Beef, pork, and lamb have long been mainstay meats in the Southwest. With endless miles of ranches supplying bountiful beef, it has been particularly popular in many chile-seasoned dishes.

With the mission of this book being quick and easy dishes, a number of popular recipes containing meat are not included. They are prepared from cuts that require long, slow simmering, which we don't have time for here.

Pork was introduced to the Southwest by the Spanish and is the mainstay in a number of traditional dishes. Here I have used the quicker-cooking cuts—pork chops and tenderloin.

The lamb fajitas and jalapeño-glazed chops are a perfect symphony of flavors. Garlic and spices are delicious with lamb.

Chile Rubbed, Grilled Rib Eye Steak

Add a chile rub and, if desired, a quick topping of green chiles and sautéed mushrooms for a feisty flavor. Prepared from start to finish in about 15 minutes, this steak is certainly wonderful enough for your favorite meat eaters.

COOKING TIME: 13 minutes for medium rare
YIELD: 3 or 4 servings

1 1/2 to 2 pounds (1-inch-thick) rib eye steaks
  1/2 medium lemon
    2 teaspoons ground pure hot red chile
    2 cloves garlic, minced
      Freshly ground black pepper

Trim any excess fat off the edge of the meat. To prevent curling, cut every 2 inches about 1/4 inch deep into the flesh. Prepare the outdoor grill, or preheat the broiler or stovetop grill to high.

Squeeze the lemon on both sides of each steak. In a small bowl combine the chile and garlic and rub half of the mixture on each side of the steak. Add several grinds of pepper to each. Cook for 7 minutes on one side and 6 minutes on the other. Serve at once.

VARIATION: While grilling the steak, sauté 6 to 8 mushrooms in a Tablespoon of butter until soft; top the steak before serving. For a delicious garnish, add warm parched green chile (fresh, frozen, or canned) to the top of the steak.

Flank Steak Soft Tacos

Spiced rare flank strips nestled in fresh, warm tortillas—either corn or flour—make a delicious light meal. Add shredded lettuce and salsa if you like.

COOKING TIME: 8 minutes
YIELD: 4 servings

1 1/2 pounds flank steak
1/4 cup red wine vinegar
2 cloves fresh garlic, minced
2 Tablespoons crushed caribe red chile
8 corn or wheat-flour tortillas
2 cups woodland greens, shredded romaine, or red leaf lettuce, optional
Salsa, optional

Trim the beef, then lightly score both sides in a crisscross pattern. In a small bowl combine the vinegar, garlic, and chile and rub on each side of the steak. Allow to set for about 10 minutes.

Preheat the grill, stovetop grill, broiler, or a heavy, seasoned skillet. Grill the steak for 4 minutes per side for medium rare. Meanwhile, warm the tortillas (see page 2). To serve, cut the steak into thin strips on a diagonal. Each guest can roll up slices of the beef in a tortilla and top it with lettuce and salsa, if desired.

PER SERVING (2 tacos): Calories 403, Protein 39 g, Carbohydrates 28 g, Fiber 4 g, Fat 15 g, Saturated Fat 6 g, Cholesterol 88 mg, Sodium 197 mg (Analyzed with corn tortillas.)

Southwestern Burgers

A big favorite in New Mexico is a juicy hamburger topped with green chile. If you want to go all out, you can add Cheddar and Monterey Jack cheeses. In fact, there are lots of Green Chile Cheeseburger contests and "Throw Downs" at the New Mexico State Fair and for fund-raisers. Some folks add guacamole, bacon, and even corn chips crushed over the guac. Other favorite toppings are salsa and refried beans.

COOKING TIME: 10 to 12 minutes
YIELD: 4 servings

- 1 teaspoon salt
   Several grinds of black pepper
- 2 pounds lean ground beef (90 percent lean, such as ground sirloin or round)
- 4 hamburger buns
- 1/2 cup chopped green chiles or 1 (4-ounce) can green chiles

OPTIONAL TOPPINGS

Shredded Cheddar and Monterey Jack cheeses
Crisply fried bacon
Guacamole
Crushed corn chips
Refried beans

Preheat the grill, if using. Add salt and pepper to the ground beef and mix well. Shape into 4 patties, making sure the edges are uniformly thick and smooth.

If pan-searing, heat a heavy, well-seasoned skillet. Add the burgers to the hot grill or skillet and cook for 5 to 6 minutes per side, to the desired doneness. If desired, toast the buns on the grill or in the skillet 2 to 3 minutes before the burgers are done. Top the burgers with the green chile about a minute before they are done. Place the burgers on the bottom half of the buns. Add toppings as desired.

PER SERVING: Calories 423, Protein 39 g, Carbohydrates 24 g, Fiber 1 g, Fat 18 g, Saturated Fat 7 g, Cholesterol 62 mg, Sodium 970 mg

Beef Enchilada Bake

This hearty favorite is a wonderful make-ahead dish. You can prepare several and have them on hand in the freezer. In New Mexico, enchiladas are generally served flat, as suggested here.

COOKING TIME: 17 to 20 minutes
YIELD: 4 servings

- 1 pound ground chuck (80 percent lean)
- 2 cups Basic Red Chile Sauce (recipe on page 156)
- 8 corn tortillas
- 1/2 cup chopped onion
- 1 cup shredded Cheddar and Monterey Jack cheeses
  Lettuce for garnish
  Chopped tomato for garnish

Sauté the beef in a heavy skillet over medium heat, breaking up all lumps and cooking for about 5 minutes, or until the pink color is almost gone. Drain off any visible fat. Add the chile sauce to the beef (or make it in the same skillet with the beef, omitting the fat and adding the flour to the drained beef, then the chile powder, then stirring in the stock and seasonings).

Preheat the oven to 375°F (190°C). Using an 8 x 10- or 9 x 9-inch baking dish or pan, pour in some of the meat sauce, then a layer of 4 tortillas, then more sauce, half the onion, and half the shredded cheeses. Add the remaining 4 tortillas, sauce, onion, and cheeses. Bake for 12 to 15 minutes, until the cheese bubbles and the mixture cooks together. Serve garnished with the lettuce and chopped tomato.

PER SERVING: Calories 531, Protein 32 g, Carbohydrates 38 g, Fiber 7 g, Fat 29 g, Saturated Fat 14 g, Cholesterol 108 mg, Sodium 677 mg
PER SERVING: Calories 469, Protein 37 g, Carbohydrates 38 g, Fiber 7 g, Fat 19 g, Saturated Fat 8 g, Cholesterol 63 mg, Sodium 727 mg (Analyzed using 91 percent lean beef and low-fat cheese.)

Salsa Beef Stir Fry

Corn, salsa, and beef are all-American, all-Southwestern. Most any kind of salad—tossed green, coleslaw, or fruit—will complement this quick meal in one dish.

COOKING TIME: 13 to 15 minutes
YIELD: 4 servings

- 1 pound extra-lean ground beef (92 percent lean)*
- 1 cup tomato-based salsa
- 1 (15 1/4-ounce) can whole kernel corn, drained, or 1 (10-ounce) package frozen
- 8 ounces dry, uncooked pasta (blue corn, green chile, or plain fusilli)**
  Shredded Cheddar and Monterey Jack cheeses, optional

Sauté the beef in a heavy, nonstick skillet, making sure no lumps remain. Drain off any visible fat. To the beef add the salsa, corn, and pasta. Stir well to coat the pasta. Cover and simmer for 6 to 8 minutes or until done. Taste and adjust the seasonings. Serve with a side dish of the shredded cheeses, if desired.

* Round steak cut into thin strips, such as for Asian dishes, is a good substitute for the ground beef, if preferred.
** You can use most any kind of pasta—even spaghetti or capellini broken into 3- to 4-inch lengths. Using leftover cooked pasta will shorten the cooking time.

PER SERVING: Calories 455, Protein 33 g, Carbohydrates 56 g, Fiber 5 g, Fat 12 g, Saturated Fat 4 g, Cholesterol 41 mg, Sodium 255 mg

Seared Chile Pork Tossed with Pasta

Chilied pork bites nestled in pasta is a fast, fun, and yummy meal with a simple tossed salad on the side. Pretty enough for company, this dish can be ready in twenty minutes or less. This is a "Sunday Best" recipe.

COOKING TIME: 8 to 10 minutes
YIELD: 4 servings

- 12 ounces pork tenderloin
- 1 Tablespoon Basic Rub (recipe on page 173)
- 1 Tablespoon unsalted butter
- 3 cloves garlic, minced
- 1/4 cup nonfat sour cream
- 1/2 cup tomato-based salsa
- 10 ounces fusilli, cooked (can be a flavored pasta, such as cilantro, jalapeño, or blue corn)

Trim the pork of all fat and sinew and cut it into 3/4-inch squares. To coat the pieces of pork, shake them with the rub in a plastic bag or toss them in a bowl.

Heat a well-seasoned, heavy skillet. Add butter and garlic. When garlic becomes clear, add the pork cubes. Cook quickly on medium-high heat to brown all sides. Cook pork until crisp on the outside and juicy inside. Stir in the sour cream and salsa. When well blended, add the pasta and toss together and serve.

PER SERVING: Calories 262, Protein 23 g, Carbohydrates 26 g, Fiber 2 g, Fat 7 g, Saturated Fat 3 g, Cholesterol 59 mg, Sodium 662 mg

Las Cruces Pork with Zippy Glaze

Pork tenderloins cook quickly, are low in fat, and are complemented by spicy flavors. When I was a child, my Mexican aunt introduced me to the symphony of flavors possible when orange, chiles, and cumin were married with pork. This dish is a quick and easy version of hers.

COOKING TIME: 10 to 12 minutes
YIELD: 2 to 4 servings

- 1   teaspoon freshly ground cumin
- 1   teaspoon coarsely ground pepper (black, white, pink, or green)
- 1/4 teaspoon salt
- 12 ounces pork tenderloin, fat and sinew removed
- 1/2 cup (1/2 recipe) Zippy Glaze (recipe on page 172)

Preheat the oven to 450°F (230°C). In a small bowl combine the cumin, pepper, and salt. Rub over the pork. Place the pork in the oven and roast for 8 to 10 minutes, until it reaches an internal temperature of 165°F (75°C) and is somewhat springy when pressed. Test for doneness by inserting a knife into the most dense part. The meat should be slightly pink.

Spoon half the glaze smoothly over the top. Roast a minute. Turn roast and spoon remaining sauce over roast and return it to the oven for about a minute. Then remove from the oven and let stand for at least 5 minutes before serving so the juices can set up. Spoon sauce from pan on each plate and arrange slices over sauce in a circular pattern.

PER SERVING (1/4 recipe): Calories 223, Protein 19 g, Carbohydrates 31 g, Fiber 1 g, Fat 4 g, Saturated Fat 1 g, Cholesterol 50 mg, Sodium 279 mg

Chile Sage Pork Chops

These pungent flavors are wonderful to come home to. Fresh sage is far better than dried in this dish. Grilling the chops over mesquite enhances the Southwestern taste, but you can broil or pan broil them instead. Serve them with Black-Eyed Pea Salsa (recipe on page 170) and Chipotle and Roasted Garlic Mashed Potatoes (recipe on page 103) for a real Southwestern treat.

COOKING TIME: 10 to 16 minutes
YIELD: 4 servings

    8 large cloves garlic, minced
    1 Tablespoon extra-virgin olive oil, preferably Spanish
  1/4 cup fresh sage leaves, minced
    2 Tablespoons ground pure hot red New Mexican chile
    4 (1/2- to 1-inch-thick) large pork chops, trimmed, rinsed, and patted dry
       Black-Eyed Pea Salsa (recipe on page 170), optional
       Chipotle and Roasted Garlic Mashed Potatoes (recipe on page 103), optional

If grilling, prepare the grill. Using a mini-chopper, puree the garlic. Add the oil and sage and grind finely. Place the mixture in a small bowl and stir in the chile. Evenly coat both sides of the chops with the mixture and rub it in. Grill or broil the chops, or pan-sear them in a hot, heavy skillet. Cook for 5 to 8 minutes per side for medium well, until the meat is light pink and registers 165°F (75°C) on a meat thermometer. If desired, serve with Black-Eyed Pea Salsa and mashed potatoes.

PER SERVING: Calories 264, Protein 26 g, Carbohydrates 5 g, Fiber 2 g, Fat 15 g, Saturated Fat 5 g, Cholesterol 70 mg, Sodium 53 mg

Aztec-Style Pork Chops

We have the Aztecs to thank for chipotle chiles. With their spicy, smoky taste, they are delicious combined with cinnamon in this dish. Serve them with grilled jicama for crunch, whipped sweet potatoes with carrots, and a spinach salad for a meal fine enough for company. This is a "Sunday Best" recipe.

COOKING TIME: 16 minutes
YIELD: 4 servings

2	dried chipotle chiles, reconstituted (see page 59) and drained, or 1 teaspoon ground chipotle
4	cloves garlic, minced
1/4	cup honey
1 1/2	teaspoons ground cinnamon
1	Tablespoon ground pure mild red chile
4	(1-inch-thick) pork loin chops, trimmed of excess fat
4	slices jicama, each 1/4 inch thick
4	cinnamon sticks

In a shallow bowl combine the chiles, garlic, honey, ground cinnamon, and ground chile. Add enough chipotle cooking liquid to make a thick paste. Marinate for 10 to 15 minutes.

Preheat the grill, stovetop grill, or a large, heavy, seasoned skillet to medium-high. Grill the chops for 8 minutes per side. At the same time and on the same surface, grill the jicama until it is slightly edged with brown on each side. To serve, top each chop with a cinnamon stick. Overlap each chop with a slice of the grilled jicama.

PER SERVING: Calories 281, Protein 25 g, Carbohydrates 20 g, Fiber 1 g, Fat 11 g, Saturated Fat 4 g, Cholesterol 70 mg, Sodium 53 mg

Grilled Veal Chops with Fruited Salsa

The tender, delicate flavor of veal is complemented by fruit with a "kick"—chile. If you are grilling the veal outdoors, grill vegetables to go along with it, such as sweet potatoes with honey butter and zucchini or asparagus with lime and chile.

COOKING TIME: 10 minutes
YIELD: 4 servings

4　(3/4-inch-thick) veal chops, trimmed of excess fat
1　Tablespoon extra-virgin olive oil, preferably Spanish
2　cloves garlic, minced
　　Several grinds of pepper (green peppercorns, if available)
1　recipe Fruited Salsa (approximately 1 cup) (recipe on page 169)

Rinse the veal, pat dry, and set aside. In a small bowl combine the oil, garlic, and ground pepper. Rub seasoning mixture evenly on both sides of each chop. Preheat the grill, stovetop grill, or a heavy, seasoned skillet until hot. Grill the chops for 4 to 5 minutes per side. Serve napped with the salsa.

PER SERVING: Calories 250, Protein 30 g, Carbohydrates 15 g, Fiber 4 g, Fat 8 g, Saturated Fat 2 g, Cholesterol 91 mg, Sodium 74 mg

Lamb Fajitas

Lamb takes well to fajita flavors—lime and freshly minced garlic. (Dried garlic doesn't impart the needed fresh taste.) This is a "Sunday Best" recipe.

COOKING TIME: 4 to 6 minutes
YIELD: 4 servings

Juice of 1 lime (about 1 1/2 Tablespoons juice)
4 cloves garlic, minced
1 Tablespoon extra-virgin olive oil, preferably Spanish
Several grinds of black pepper
1 1/2 pounds leg of lamb or sirloin, sliced 1/4 inch thick
8 white-flour tortillas
Pico de Gallo (recipe on page 168) for garnish
1/2 cup sour cream for garnish

In a shallow, nonreactive bowl, combine the lime juice, garlic, oil, and ground pepper. Tenderize the lamb with a meat tenderizer tool—not chemically. Place the lamb slices, one at a time, in the lime mixture, pressing the mixture into one side of each slice, then turning the slice and pressing the mixture into the other side.

Preheat the grill, stovetop grill, or a heavy, nonstick skillet until hot. Sear the meat for 2 to 3 minutes per side. Remove and slice into 3/4-inch strips. Serve in the tortillas with pico de gallo and sour cream.

PER SERVING: Calories 784, Protein 46 g, Carbohydrates 95 g, Fiber 6 g, Fat 24 g, Saturated Fat 7 g, Cholesterol 100 mg, Sodium 795 mg (Analyzed with two 10-inch flour tortillas [substitute corn tortilla and save over 300 calories], pico de gallo, and nonfat sour cream.)

PER SERVING: Calories 251, Protein 30 g, Carbohydrates 2 g, Sodium 75 mg (Analyzed with lamb alone.)

Lamb Chops with Jalapeño Jelly

Garlicky lamb chops are delicious when scented with fresh Mexican oregano, lime, and fragrant Spanish extra-virgin olive oil. These quick-as-a-wink chops are wonderful served on a bed of white beans teased with freshly squeezed garlic, minced scallions, chopped cilantro, and extra-virgin olive oil.

COOKING TIME: 8 to 10 minutes
YIELD: 4 servings

- 8 (1-inch-thick) loin or rib lamb chops, trimmed of excess fat
- 3 cloves garlic, minced
- 1 Tablespoon chopped fresh or 1 teaspoon dried Mexican oregano
- 1 1/2 Tablespoons extra-virgin olive oil, preferably Spanish
  White Bean Salsa (recipe on page 171)
- 3 Tablespoons jalapeño jelly

Rinse the lamb chops and pat dry. In a mini-chopper or blender, place the garlic, oregano, and oil and process until smooth. Smear the mixture onto both sides of each chop as uniformly as possible.

Preheat the grill, stovetop grill, or a heavy, seasoned, nonstick skillet until hot. Grill or sear the chops for 4 to 5 minutes per side. Serve on a bed of the white bean salsa with the two chop bones vertically intertwined. Place one-fourth of the jalapeño jelly atop each pair of lamb chops.

PER SERVING: Calories 362, Protein 38 g, Carbohydrates 12 g, Fiber 1 g, Fat 17 g, Saturated Fat 6 g, Cholesterol 119 mg, Sodium 112 mg

*A "Sunday Best" recipe with more than five ingredients but fewer than ten.

MAIN DISH SALADS

With the increasing popularity of lighter main dishes, salads with a Southwestern theme are just perfect. You can combine spicy ingredients with a range of vegetables and perhaps meat or seafood. No wonder these salads have become so popular.

Here I've developed simple, light Southwestern main dish salads with low-fat dressings. Some of our favorites are the Fajita Pasta Salad (recipe on page 36), especially when it's made with red chile pasta. The spicy, fresh, lemon-edged dressing for the Caesar in a Bowl (recipe on page 37) pleased my anchovy-loving husband, Gordon, even though the salad had less than half the amount of anchovy-laden dressing I normally use. The Grilled Chicken and Chard Salad (recipe on page 39) is pretty as a picture and flavorful too.

The Chicken Rice Salad with Jalapeño Lime Creme Dressing (recipe on page 40) prompted him to say I had outdone myself. A true Texan, he thought the Spicy Beef 'n Potato Salad (recipe on page 42) was hard to beat. You can see we really did enjoy developing these salads for you.

Fajita Pasta Salad

Using leftover marinated meat from fajitas makes this salad quick to prepare. I like to make fajitas of all sorts—beef, chicken, shrimp, even lamb and duck (pages 32 and 138)—and freeze one-person servings in freezer-weight bags, complete with the marinade. My favorite basic recipe, which can be used with any meat or seafood, is on page 138. This pasta salad is a "Sunday Best" recipe.

COOKING TIME: 15 minutes
YIELD: 4 servings

1/2	recipe Fajita Favorites (meat only), either beef, chicken, or shrimp (recipe on page 138)
5	ounces dry, uncooked fusilli or rigatoni pasta, preferably chile flavored
1	cup home-cooked or drained canned pinto beans
4	scallions, white and tender green tops, thinly sliced
2	red ripe Roma tomatoes, chopped
1/4	cup spicy salad dressing: choose from Hotter-Than-Fire Dressing (recipe on page 38), Jalapeño Lime Creme Dressing (recipe on page 48), or Hot Red Chile Dressing (recipe on page 43) Torn lettuces, optional

Preferably, have the meat for the fajitas previously marinated, or prepare it and set aside. Preheat the outdoor grill or soak wood chips for the indoor stovetop grill (we like mesquite). Bring a large pot of salted water to a boil and cook the pasta according to package directions. Drain in a colander and set aside.

Grill the meat or pan-sear it in a heavy, seasoned skillet. Cook for 2 to 3 minutes per side for beef or shrimp, 4 to 5 minutes per side for chicken. Slice the beef or chicken into 1/2-inch-wide strips (leave shrimp whole). In a large bowl combine the pasta with the beans, scallions, tomatoes, and meat. Add the salad dressing and toss together. If desired, arrange each serving on a bed of torn lettuces. Serve at room temperature.

PER SERVING: Calories 351, Protein 26 g, Carbohydrates 39 g, Fiber 6 g, Fat 10 g, Saturated Fat 3 g, Cholesterol 44 mg, Sodium 205 mg (Analyzed with beef fajitas and Hotter-Than-Fire Dressing.)

Caesar in a Bowl

Legend has it that the original Caesar salad was created in Tijuana, Mexico, by Caesar Cardini in 1924 to commemorate the special visit of a Hollywood movie star. Cardini was the chef of one of the prominent hotels in Tijuana.

This spicy version of the salad is not as heavy with anchovies or oil as the popular restaurant versions. Use deli or leftover turkey or chicken. If preferred, lime- and garlic-accented chicken breast (fajita style) could be quickly grilled, sliced, and added instead. The salad is also wonderful without any chicken or turkey. It is a "Sunday Best" recipe.

PREPARATION TIME: 15 minutes
YIELD: 4 servings

1	large head romaine lettuce, about 12 ounces
6	Tablespoons freshly squeezed lemon juice (about 2 lemons)
1 or 2	fresh jalapeño chiles, minced (add second jalapeño after tasting if desired)
3	cloves garlic, minced
4	anchovy fillets, drained and mashed, or 2 teaspoons anchovy paste
1/4	cup extra-virgin olive oil, preferably Spanish
2	cups (1/2-inch) cubed turkey or chicken breast
1/4	cup freshly grated Parmesan or Romano cheese, optional

Rinse the lettuce, drain, and tear into bite-size pieces; chill. In a deep salad bowl, combine the lemon juice, jalapeños, garlic, anchovies, and oil. Using a whisk or a fork, blend them together (or use a mini-chopper to blend all together). Add the lettuce and turkey and toss to mix. Top with the cheese, if desired.

PER SERVING: Calories 252, Protein 25 g, Carbohydrates 5 g, Fiber 2 g, Fat 15 g, Saturated Fat 2 g, Cholesterol 64 mg, Sodium 194 mg (Analyzed with turkey, 12 ounces of romaine lettuce, and 1 1/2 jalapeños.)

Hotter-Than-Fire Dressing

This salad dressing delivers what it promises. Tightly covered, it will keep one month in the refrigerator.

PREPARATION TIME: 5 minutes
YIELD: 1 cup

- 3/4 cup spicy hot tomato juice (approximately 1 [5 1/2-ounce] can)
- 3 Tablespoons cider vinegar
- 1 fresh jalapeño chile, minced
- 1 teaspoon crushed red pequin quebrado chile
- 2 cloves garlic, minced
- 2 Tablespoons extra-virgin olive oil, preferably Spanish

In a bowl combine the tomato juice, vinegar, jalapeño, pequin chile, garlic, and oil. Whisk together, or place in a jar and shake.

PER SERVING (2 Tablespoons): Calories 38, Protein 0 g, Carbohydrates 2 g, Fiber 0 g, Fat 3 g, Saturated Fat 0 g, Cholesterol 0 mg, Sodium 83 mg

Grilled Chicken and Chard Salad

Grilled chicken breast is the darling of the new trend toward fast, low-fat meals. It is quick and easy to prepare and is stunning with the chard, which you can prepare easily on a stovetop grill.

COOKING TIME: 10 to 12 minutes
YIELD: 2 large or 4 small servings

2	(6-ounce) boneless, skinless chicken breast halves
1	teaspoon Basic Rub (recipe on page 173)
1	bunch of red, multicolored, or white Swiss chard (12 to 16 ounces)
1	large Spanish-style white onion (if red chard unavailable, substitute red onion)
1/4	cup Cilantro Salsa (recipe on page 165) or Tomatillo Salsa (recipe on page 160)

Trim the chicken, removing all fat and membrane. Rinse, pat dry, and evenly sprinkle with rub and rub into surfaces of chicken. Rinse the chard and cut into 2-inch-wide strips. Slice the onion in half lengthwise, then cut it crosswise into 1/2-inch-wide strips.

Preheat a large, heavy, well-seasoned skillet until hot. If necessary, spray the skillet with nonstick oil. Grill the onion for about 3 minutes; do not stir until the edges blacken somewhat. Stir and push the onions to the side and add the chicken breast. Cook for 4 minutes, then turn the chicken and cook for another 4 minutes.

When the onion is somewhat soft and the edges are browned, remove from the skillet. Place the chard in the skillet off to one side. Check for chicken doneness by pressing with your finger. The chicken should be firm to the touch and, when sliced, white inside. Remove the chicken to a cutting board. Cover the skillet and sear the chard until some of the leaves are blackened and wilted on the edges.

To serve, arrange the chard in a strip down the center of each plate. Arrange the onion in a row on each side of the chard. Cut the chicken into 1/2-inch-wide slices and center it in a row on the chard. Top with the salsa.

PER SERVING (1/4 recipe): Calories 138, Protein 20 g, Carbohydrates 10 g, Fiber 3 g, Fat 2 g, Saturated Fat 1 g, Cholesterol 47 mg, Sodium 308 mg (Analyzed with Cilantro Salsa.)

— **Chicken Rice Salad with Jalapeño Lime Creme Dressing** —

With the use of a convenient Southwestern-flavored rice mix and deli chicken, this salad goes together in nothing flat. Serve with garlic buttered tortillas, either corn or flour.

COOKING TIME: 10 to 12 minutes
YIELD: 4 servings

    1 (6-ounce) package Southwestern-flavored rice mix
3/4 pound boneless, skinless deli chicken, diced
    1 (4-ounce) can diced green chiles
    1 red bell pepper, diced
1/4 cup Jalapeño Lime Creme Dressing (recipe on page 48)
1/4 cup sliced ripe olives for garnish
    1 head of red or green leaf lettuce, rinsed and torn into bite-size pieces for garnish

Cook the rice according to package directions. Set aside to cool. Place the chicken, chiles, pepper, and rice in a large bowl and toss with the salad dressing. Add the olives, if desired. To serve, divide the salad onto 4 plates, on top of the lettuce, if using.

PER SERVING: Calories 333, Protein 32 g, Carbohydrates 38 g, Fiber 4 g, Fat 7 g, Saturated Fat 3 g, Cholesterol 80 mg, Sodium 767 mg (Analyzed with 1 Tablespoon butter called for in the package of rice mix.)

Spinach, Shrimp, and Pear Salad with Piñons

The fresh, healthy taste of spinach is perfect with pears for a change from the predictable lettuces. Small shrimp and Hotter-Than-Fire Dressing (recipe on page 38) make it wonderful. Garlic or cheese breadsticks would make a good accompaniment to this salad.

PREPARATION TIME: 6 to 8 minutes
YIELD: 2 large or 4 small servings

- 2 ripe Bartlett or D'Anjou pears
- 1 (12-ounce) package fresh spinach, washed and dried
- 3/4 pound small, cooked shrimp, peeled and deveined
- 1/4 cup Hotter-Than-Fire Dressing (recipe on page 38)
  Freshly ground black pepper, optional
- 2 Tablespoons roasted piñons*

Slice the pears in half lengthwise; remove the core (but leave the peel), then cut the fruit into thin wedges. Place the spinach and shrimp in a salad bowl and toss with the dressing. Add ground pepper, if desired. To serve, divide the spinach mixture among the plates or bowls and top with the pear wedges. Sprinkle with the piñons and serve.

* If roasted piñons (pine nuts) are unavailable, roast them in a sauté pan over medium-high heat, stirring and watching carefully—they burn very easily.

Spicy Beef 'n Potato Salad

Combined with baby red potatoes and caramelized onions, this makes a satisfying meal for the beef-and-potatoes set but is light enough to please the weight conscious too. This is a "Sunday Best" recipe.

COOKING TIME: 20 minutes
YIELD: 4 servings

3/4	pound beef sirloin tip, well-trimmed
1	teaspoon Basic Rub (recipe on page 173)
1 1/2	pounds baby red potatoes, well-scrubbed
2	teaspoons unsalted butter, divided
1	large onion, halved and thinly sliced into rings
2	cups mixed baby greens
1/4	cup Hot Red Chile Dressing (recipe on page 43)

Using a tenderizer mallet, pound the beef to about 1/4 inch thick. Add the rub to both sides of the beef. Place the potatoes in boiling salted water, cover, and cook for 12 to 15 minutes, until fork-tender. Drain the potatoes and add 1 teaspoon of the butter; stir and cover.

In a well-seasoned or nonstick skillet over medium heat, place the remaining 1 teaspoon of the butter and coat the bottom of the pan. Add the onion; cover and cook for about 3 minutes, stirring occasionally, until the onions start to sweat and become limp. Uncover and cook for about another 2 minutes, or until golden, stirring occasionally. Remove the onions from the pan. Increase the heat to high and add the beef. Sauté for about 1 1/2 minutes per side for medium-rare beef, which is the juiciest. Remove to a cutting board and let the beef rest.

Cut the beef into 1/4-inch-thick slices, then cut each slice into 2-inch lengths. Place in a salad bowl. Add the potatoes, onion, greens, and dressing; toss together. Serve immediately.

PER SERVING (1/4 recipe): Calories 314, Protein 23 g, Carbohydrates 36 g, Fiber 4 g, Fat 9 g, Saturated Fat 4 g, Cholesterol 58 mg, Sodium 229 mg

Hot Red Chile Dressing

This dressing has a wine base rather than the spicy tomato one used in Hotter-Than-Fire Dressing. It will keep at least a month in the refrigerator.

PREPARATION TIME: 5 minutes
YIELD: 1/2 cup (enough for 1 4-serving salad)

- 1/4 cup dry white wine
- 2 large cloves garlic, minced
- 1 Tablespoon Dijon mustard
- 2 Tablespoons red wine or balsamic vinegar
- 1 Tablespoon extra-virgin olive oil, preferably Spanish

In a small bowl combine the wine, garlic, mustard, vinegar, and oil. Whisk together, or place in a jar and shake.

PER SERVING (1/4 recipe): Calories 47, Protein 0 g, Carbohydrates 1 g, Fiber 0 g, Fat 4 g, Saturated Fat 0 g, Cholesterol 0 mg, Sodium 97 mg

Smoked Trout with Seashell Pasta

Most delis have smoked trout, or you can quick-smoke one. This salad is filling when paired with sour-dough bread dipped in olive oil.

COOKING TIME: 10 to 15 minutes
YIELD: 4 servings

10	ounces dry, uncooked seashell pasta or other medium-size pasta, such as bow tie
1	(8-ounce) smoked trout, skinned, boned, and broken into large flakes*
4	scallions, white and tender green parts, thinly sliced
1/4	cup sliced ripe olives
1/2	cup (1/2 recipe) Jalapeño Lime Creme Dressing (recipe on page 48) or Spicy Cilantro Lime Dressing (recipe on page 48)
	Caribe chile flakes for garnish
	A few salad greens for garnish

Bring a large pot of salted water to a boil and cook the pasta according to package directions. Drain, then run ice water through the pasta. Drain again and place in a salad bowl. Add the trout, scallions, and olives. Toss with the dressing and garnish with a light sprinkle of caribe chile flakes. Tuck a few salad greens into the edge of the bowl.

* To quick-smoke a fresh trout, you will need a few wood chips or a bag of black tea, a heavy pot, and a rack to hold the trout. Preheat the oven to 425°F (220°C). Salt and pepper the inside and outside of the trout. Place the chips or tea in the bottom of the pot. Cover and place over medium-high heat. In 5 to 7 minutes, when the wood chips or tea begin to smoke, lower the trout on a rack in the pan, over the chips, and cover. Smoke for 15 minutes.

PER SERVING: Calories 423, Protein 28 g, Carbohydrates 61 g, Fiber 3 g, Fat 7 g, Saturated Fat 2 g, Cholesterol 45 mg, Sodium 1234 mg

Terrific Scallop Tostado Salad

Home-baked tostado chips are fresher tasting than store-bought, but you can use either. Or you can use an assortment of corn and wheat- or white-flour tortillas. Using a seasoned rub on the scallops before searing gives them a Southwestern "bite."

COOKING TIME: 4 minutes
YIELD: 4 servings

- 1 pound bay scallops
- 2 teaspoons Basic Rub (recipe on page 173) or favorite commercial rub
- 6 cups salad greens
- 4 Tablespoons Jalapeño Lime Creme Dressing (recipe on page 48) or Spicy Cilantro Lime Dressing (recipe on page 48)
- 16 baked corn tortilla tostados or Tortilla Toasts (4 corn tortillas) (recipe on page 6)

Rinse the scallops and pat dry with a paper towel. Place the scallops on a paper plate, sprinkle with the rub, and toss to coat.

Preheat a heavy, seasoned, nonstick skillet over medium-high heat; spray the skillet with nonstick spray if necessary. Quickly sear the scallops, stirring a few times to cook evenly, for 1 1/2 to 2 minutes, just until done. They will seize up as they cook yet should still be moist and tender.

To serve, divide the salad greens evenly among the plates, top each with the scallops, and drizzle each with 1 Tablespoon of the dressing. Stab tostado triangles into the top, bottom, and each side of the salad at the 6, 9, 12, and 3 o'clock positions. Serve warm.

PER SERVING: Calories 145, Protein 13 g, Carbohydrates 18 g, Fiber 3 g, Fat 3 g, Saturated Fat 0 g, Cholesterol 18 mg, Sodium 640 mg

Carne Adobado Stir-Fried Slaw

Strange-sounding name? Carne adobado is actually a favorite traditional northern New Mexican pork dish that was conquistador inspired. Pork and chiles were meant for each other. Because this salad combines spice, crunch, and color, you may want to serve it solo or precede it with a cup of creamy soup, such as Chicken Tortilla Chowder (recipe on page 100) or Chile-Sparked Sweet Potato Soup (recipe on page 94). This slaw is a "Sunday Best" recipe.

COOKING TIME: 5 to 7 minutes in a microwave oven, 13 to 14 minutes in a conventional oven
YIELD: 4 servings

1	(1 1/4 pound) pork tenderloin
1/4	cup crushed red caribe chile or ground pure mild red chile for a milder flavor
1	large clove garlic
1	teaspoon Mexican oregano
1	teaspoon freshly ground cumin
3	cups shredded coleslaw base, preferably red cabbage, or hand-shredded red cabbage
1/3	cup cider vinegar

Trim the tenderloin of any fat and sinew-like casing. Cut the meat into slices about 1/4 inch thick.

In a blender, place 3/4 cup water and add the chile, garlic, oregano, and cumin. Process until thick. Pour the mixture into a 1-quart microwavable baking pan.* Add the pork slices and stir to mix. Cover with wax paper and cook in the microwave oven for 5 minutes. Stir, check the pork for doneness, and cook for 2 more minutes if needed, or until the pink color disappears.

Add the cabbage and vinegar and stir to mix. Taste for flavor balance, adjusting if necessary. Cover again with the wax paper and cook for 2 minutes. To serve, arrange the cabbage on the plates and top with the pork strips.

* For stovetop cooking, place the pork and the sauce in a deep skillet or a 5-quart Dutch oven. Bring to a simmer and cook for 10 minutes, or until the pork is no longer pink. Add the cabbage and vinegar, cover, and cook for 3 to 4 minutes, until the cabbage is slightly wilted.

PER SERVING: Calories 210, Protein 31 g, Carbohydrates 7 g, Fiber 3 g, Fat 6 g, Saturated Fat 2 g, Cholesterol 84 mg, Sodium 73 mg

Grilled Vegetable Salad

Vegetables are wonderful fresh off the grill and made into a salad. Or you can use grilled vegetables left over from a day or so before. For a salad, I like grilled corn, red bell peppers, onions, green chiles, and eggplant. Other vegetables such as black beans and greens can be combined with them. This is a "Sunday Best" recipe.

COOKING TIME: 8 to 10 minutes
YIELD: 4 servings

  2 large or 3 medium ears fresh corn, husked
  1 large red bell pepper
  1 large red onion, cut into 1/4-inch slices
  3 fresh green chiles, parched (instructions on page xvii), or 1 (4-ounce) can chopped green chiles
  1 (15-ounce) can black beans, drained
  4 cups mesclun or woodland greens, well-rinsed
1/2 cup Jalapeño Lime Creme Dressing (recipe on page 48) or Hotter-Than-Fire Dressing (recipe on page 38)
    Corn chips, preferably blue corn, optional

Preheat an outdoor grill, stovetop grill, or broiler to medium-high heat.

Place the corn, red pepper, onion slices, and fresh chiles on the grill.* Cook for 8 to 10 minutes, rotating them as they blister, until they are uniformly charred on the edges. The onion slices should be almost soft.

Cut the corn off the cob. Place the red pepper and green chiles in ice water, then peel and chop into 1/2-inch dice. Coarsely chop the onion into 1/2-inch dice. Place corn, red pepper, chiles, and onions in a bowl and toss with the black beans and greens. Add the dressing, toss lightly, and serve. Garnish with the corn chips, if using.

* If you are using canned chiles, add them with the black beans.

PER SERVING: Calories 225, Protein 14 g, Carbohydrates 43 g, Fiber 10 g, Fat 2 g, Saturated Fat 0 g, Cholesterol 1 mg, Sodium 403 mg

All of the following salad dressings are low in fat and quick to make.
Or you may choose to purchase low- or nonfat commercial salad dressings.

Jalapeño Lime Creme Dressing

The combination of flavors is perfect for a wide range of salads as well as for a sauce to serve with meats or vegetables.

PREPARATION TIME: 5 minutes
YIELD: 1 cup

1	cup plain yogurt or 3/4 cup nonfat sour cream with 1/4 cup skim milk whisked in
1 or 2	fresh jalapeño chiles, minced
1/4	cup coarsely chopped cilantro
2	teaspoons freshly squeezed lime juice (1/2 lime)
1/2	teaspoon lime zest

In a bowl combine the yogurt, jalapeños, cilantro, lime juice, and zest. Whisk together, or place in a jar and shake. This dressing will keep at least 2 weeks covered in the refrigerator.

PER SERVING (2 Tablespoons): Calories 20, Protein 2 g, Carbohydrates 3 g, Fiber 0 g, Fat 0 g, Saturated Fat 0 g, Cholesterol 1 mg, Sodium 24 mg

Spicy Cilantro Lime Dressing

This dressing is particularly good on a spinach and red onion salad or any combination of greens.

PREPARATION TIME: 5 minutes
YIELD: 1/2 cup (enough for 1 4-serving salad)

3	Tablespoons freshly squeezed lime juice (1 or 2 limes)
1	Tablespoon honey, preferably desert blossom
1	Tablespoon coarsely chopped fresh cilantro
1/2	fresh jalapeño chile, minced
	Pinch of salt, optional

In a small bowl combine the lime juice, honey, cilantro, and jalapeño. Whisk until well blended.*
Taste and adjust the seasonings, adding salt, if needed.

* If you have a mini-chopper, use it to mince the jalapeño and combine all the ingredients.

PER SERVING (1/4 recipe): Calories 21, Protein 0 g, Carbohydrates 6 g, Fiber 0 g, Fat 0 g, Saturated Fat 0 g, Cholesterol 0 mg, Sodium 1 mg

——— Creamy Ranch-Style Dressing ———

This version of ranch dressing is very low fat and tasty, with the tang of yogurt edged with low-fat mayonnaise and flavored with herbs.

PREPARATION TIME: 5 minutes
YIELD: 1 cup

3/4 cup plain nonfat yogurt
1/4 cup low-fat mayonnaise
  1 Tablespoon cider vinegar or white vinegar
  1 Tablespoon Dijon mustard
  2 teaspoons minced fresh or 1 teaspoon crushed dried thyme
  1 scallion, white and tender green parts, minced

In a small bowl combine the yogurt, mayonnaise, vinegar, mustard, thyme, and scallion. Whisk together to combine well. Refrigerate for an hour or more before serving.

VARIATION: For another excellent dressing, substitute honey for the vinegar and tarragon for the thyme.

PER SERVING (2 Tablespoons): Calories 41, Protein 2 g, Carbohydrates 3 g, Fiber 0 g, Fat 3 g, Saturated Fat 1 g, Cholesterol 0 mg, Sodium 120 mg

*A "Sunday Best" recipe with more than five ingredients but fewer than ten.

SOUTHWESTERN PIZZA AND PASTA

The recipes in this chapter are very innovative. Favorite Italian dishes take on Southwestern pizzazz. A corn or wheat tortilla is an instant crust for most any kind of pizza. Topping ideas can come from your favorite flavors or what you have on hand. Pizzas are best grilled, broiled, or skillet-seared on top of the range. A microwave oven will work, but it does not give the customary crisp crust.

Pasta has gone Southwestern. Chile and other favorite Southwestern flavors such as cilantro, sun-dried tomato, and blue corn are popular. I have called for these in some of the recipes because the spicy flavor and attractive color make the dish even more special. Lacking these, you do not have to abandon the dish; just make it with regular pasta and perhaps compensate by adding more chiles.

Being fond of all kinds of pasta, I had a great deal of fun creating these dishes. Many can be vegetarian with just a bit of substitution, depending on the type of vegetarianism being practiced.

Tortilla Pizzas

These can be a light meal or an appetizer. They are quick to make and are a wonderful way to use what you have on hand. They are most healthful when made with corn tortillas but can be made with wheat- or white-flour tortillas, if desired. Allow one or two tortillas per person.

COOKING TIME: 2 to 3 minutes each
YIELD: 3 to 6 servings

> 6 corn tortillas
> 1 cup shredded Cheddar, Monterey Jack, or mozzarella cheese (or nonfat or goat cheese)

CHOOSE 2 OR MORE OF THE FOLLOWING:

> Cooked pinto or black beans, drained or refried
> Cooked chopped beef, chicken, turkey, or pork or fried crumbled chorizo (Mexican sausage)
> Cooked crab or shrimp
> Small avocado, peeled and slivered
> Salsa of your choice or chopped tomato and onion

Preheat the oven to 425°F (220°C). Place the tortillas on a baking sheet and bake them for 6 to 8 minutes, until crisp. Divide the cheese among the tortillas. Add your choice of toppings and place back in the oven for 2 to 3 minutes, until the cheese is melted. Serve hot with additional salsa.

PER SERVING (1/6 recipe): Calories 115, Protein 5 g, Carbohydrates 12 g, Fiber 1 g, Fat 5 g, Saturated Fat 3 g, Cholesterol 15 mg, Sodium 130 g. (Analyzed with one tortilla and Cheddar cheese, toppings extra.)

Southwestern Veggie Pizza

Wheat- or white-flour tortillas make a perfect thin-crusted pizza and cut down the time needed to ready a crust. You can always vary the topping ingredients to what you like or have on hand. This is a "Sunday Best" recipe.

COOKING TIME: 15 minutes
YIELD: 4 servings

>   4 (10- to 12-inch) wheat- or white-flour tortillas
>   Olive oil spray
>   8 large fresh mushrooms, thinly sliced
>   1 cup tomato-based salsa, plus more for garnish
>   1 cup canned corn
>   1 cup shredded Monterey Jack or mozzarella cheese
>   Hot-pepper flakes, such as pequin quebrado for garnish, optional

Preheat the oven to 425°F (220°C). Place the tortillas on a large baking sheet. Spray lightly with the oil. Place in the oven for 5 minutes. Arrange the mushrooms on the tortillas and bake for 3 to 5 more minutes, until the mushrooms are lightly browned.

Meanwhile, in a bowl mix the salsa and corn together; divide the mixture among the 4 pizzas. Garnish with the cheese and return to the oven until the cheese melts. Serve immediately with more salsa or hot-pepper flakes, if desired.

PER SERVING: Calories 398, Protein 16 g, Carbohydrates 53 g, Fiber 5 g, Fat 14 g, Saturated Fat 6 g, Cholesterol 25 mg, Sodium 753 mg

PER SERVING: Calories 374, Protein 18 g, Carbohydrates 53 g, Fiber 5 g, Fat 11 g, Saturated Fat 4 g, Cholesterol 20 mg, Sodium 824 mg (Analyzed with low-fat cheese.)

Skillet Chicken Pizza

This versatile pizza is quick to make. This is a "Sunday Best" recipe.

COOKING TIME: 15 minutes
YIELD: 2 servings

1	teaspoon olive oil or olive oil spray
1 1/4	cups sliced fresh mushrooms*
1/2	cup chopped onion
1/4	cup white wine or chicken broth (can be made with dehydrated chicken granules)
2	cups chopped, cooked, skinless chicken or turkey
2	(10- to 12-inch) wheat- or white-flour tortillas
1/2	cup shredded Monterey Jack and Cheddar cheese combination
	Spicy tomato-based salsa for garnish

Heat the oil over medium-high heat in a heavy skillet just the size of the tortilla. Add the mushrooms and onion and quickly sauté for 5 to 7 minutes, until the onion becomes clear and the mushrooms are slightly brown.

Add the wine and chicken and cook, stirring, for 3 to 5 minutes, until warm. Remove the mixture to a plate. Add a tortilla and heat for a minute or two. Add half the topping, and heat until the cheese melts. Serve with the salsa.

* You can use thinly sliced zucchini, bell pepper strips, green chile, or whatever favorite vegetable you have on hand. Olives are also good.

PER SERVING: Calories 467, Protein 37 g, Carbohydrates 46 g, Fiber 4 g, Fat 12 g, Saturated Fat 4 g, Cholesterol 73 mg, Sodium 601 mg (Analyzed with low-fat cheese.)

Southwestern Barbecue Pizza

Tortilla pizzas, which I often call pizzitas, are easy to make and perfect for those who prefer a thin crust. If you wish to have a thicker crust, substitute prebaked pizza crusts, available in most supermarkets. This pizza is a delicious way to serve leftover meats or vegetables.

COOKING TIME: 8 minutes
YIELD: 2 servings

- 2 (10- to 12-inch) wheat- or white-flour tortillas
- 2 Tablespoons spicy barbecue sauce
- 1/2 cup seared, chopped vegetables, pepperoni, or cooked chicken, beef, or pork
- 1/4 cup shredded Cheddar and Monterey Jack cheeses
- 1 onion, chopped
  Crushed red caribe chile for garnish, optional

Preheat the oven to 425°F (220°C). Place the tortillas on a baking sheet and bake for 3 minutes, or until hot. Spread half the barbecue sauce on each tortilla, then top with half the vegetables or meat. Sprinkle with half the cheeses and onion. Bake for 8 minutes, or until the cheese is bubbly. Sprinkle with the chile, if using, and serve.

VARIATION: Substitute salsa for the barbecue sauce.

PER SERVING: Calories 245, Protein 11 g, Carbohydrates 50 g, Fiber 6 g, Fat 6 g, Saturated Fat 3 g, Cholesterol 14 mg, Sodium 558 mg

Penne with Snapper and Pink Tequila Sauce

You can vary this dish with other seafood if snapper is unavailable or not a favorite. Shrimp, scallops, or a mild, firm-fleshed fish such as orange roughy work well. You can make this as a pasta-based stew such as cioppino or a thicker pasta sauce, depending on your mood.

COOKING TIME: 15 to 18 minutes
YIELD: 2 servings

  1 (14 1/2-ounce) can chicken broth*
  1 pound boneless, skinless red snapper, cut into 1/2-inch cubes
1/2 cup tomato-based salsa (spiciness suited to your taste)
  6 ounces dry, uncooked penne pasta
1/4 cup tequila

Bring 3 quarts of salted water to a boil in your favorite pasta cooking pot. Meanwhile, in a sauce pot, bring the broth to a simmer; add the snapper and salsa and cook over low heat, stirring occasionally. Add the tequila. Cook the pasta according to package directions. Drain the pasta and serve the sauce over the pasta.

* For a richer, thicker sauce, use 1 cup chicken broth and add 1/2 cup half-and-half or evaporated skim milk.

PER SERVING: Calories 596, Protein 46 g, Carbohydrates 73 g, Fiber 5 g, Fat 6 g, Saturated Fat 2 g, Cholesterol 60 mg, Sodium 330 mg

Speedy Shrimp Primavera

This pretty and flavorful pasta is good served with Italian black olive bruschetta topped simply with olive oil and minced fresh herbs such as basil, thyme, and sage. This is a "Sunday Best" recipe.

COOKING TIME: 15 minutes
YIELD: 2 servings

6	ounces dry, uncooked pasta, any type
1	Tablespoon extra-virgin olive oil, preferably Spanish
2	cloves garlic, thinly sliced
1/2	pound uncooked shrimp, peeled, deveined, and butterflied (cut lengthwise)
1/4	cup dry white wine
1	cup broccoli florets (1 stalk)
2	teaspoons crushed red caribe chile flakes for garnish

Bring a large pot of salted water to a boil and begin cooking the pasta according to package directions.

Meanwhile, heat the oil in a sauté pan, then add the garlic and cook and stir for a minute or two. Add the shrimp and cook until the pink color disappears. Add the wine and about 1/2 cup hot water from the pasta pot. Remove from the heat and keep warm.

Two minutes before the pasta is supposed to be done, add the broccoli to the pasta pot to cook. When the pasta and broccoli are done, drain and return them to the pot. Stir in the shrimp sauce and serve on warmed plates. Garnish with the chile flakes.

PER SERVING: Calories 521, Protein 30 g, Carbohydrates 72 g, Fiber 4 g, Fat 9 g, Saturated Fat 1 g, Cholesterol 161 mg, Sodium 200 mg

Chicken Chile Pasta

This spicy, creamy sauce is flavored with salad dressing mix—a real time-saver. Served hot or cold, this dish is a good way to use leftover pasta or chicken.

COOKING TIME: 10 minutes
YIELD: 4 servings

10	ounces dry, uncooked red chile pasta, any shape
1	Tablespoon olive oil
1	pound chicken tenderloins, cut into 1-inch cubes
1	(1-ounce) package dry ranch salad dressing mix
1	cup buttermilk
1/4	cup coarsely chopped cilantro or sliced scallions, white and tender green parts, for garnish, optional

Bring a large pot of salted water to a boil and cook the pasta according to package directions. Meanwhile, in a skillet over medium heat, warm the oil. Toss the chicken with 2 Tablespoons of the salad dressing mix and add to the hot oil. Cook for 6 to 8 minutes, stirring occasionally, until the pink color disappears. Do not overcook.

In a bowl large enough to hold the cooked pasta, combine the remaining salad dressing mix with the buttermilk. When the pasta is done, drain, then toss with the buttermilk mixture and stir to combine well. If serving as a salad, chill the pasta mixture and the chicken. If serving hot, immediately place the pasta mixture on plates and top each with the chicken. Garnish with the cilantro or scallion, if desired.

PER SERVING: Calories 424, Protein 33 g, Carbohydrates 53 g, Fiber 2 g, Fat 8 g, Saturated Fat 2 g, Cholesterol 65 mg, Sodium 617 mg

Black Beans with Chipotle and Fusilli

Black beans did not become popular in the Southwest until relatively recently; their rich flavor takes on the spice of chiles quite well.

COOKING TIME: 10 minutes
YIELD: 4 servings

- 10 ounces dry, uncooked fusilli
- 1 (15-ounce) can black beans, drained, or 1 1/2 cups cooked beans
- 1/4 cup minced reconstituted dried chipotle chiles (2 large or 3 medium chiles)*
- 1 teaspoon cider vinegar
- 2 cloves garlic, minced
- 2 ounces queso blanco or feta cheese, crumbled

Bring a large pot of salted water to a boil and cook the pasta according to package directions. Meanwhile, in a 3-quart saucepan, combine the beans, chipotles, vinegar, and garlic and simmer. When the pasta is done, drain and place on the plates, then top with the bean mixture and the crumbled cheese.

* To reconstitute the chipotles in a microwave oven, place the pods in a 4-cup glass measuring cup. Cover with water and add 1 teaspoon cider vinegar. Cover with plastic wrap and cook for 5 minutes, on full power, or until the skin slips on the flesh. To prepare on top of the range, cook the same mixture in a small saucepan for 30 minutes, or until the skin slips on the flesh. If mincing the chiles is called for, remove the stems but leave the skin on and the seeds in. A number of chipotles can be prepared and stored in a covered glass jar in the refrigerator for at least a month.

PER SERVING: Calories 370, Protein 16 g, Carbohydrates 66 g, Fiber 8 g, Fat 5, Saturated Fat 2 g, Cholesterol 13 mg, Sodium 313 mg (Analyzed with feta cheese.)

Southwestern Siciliano Sauce for Pasta

Easy to make and serve, this favorite sauce has been a Friday-night staple since the days when we had to have something delicious, quick, and nourishing after the ride from New York City to our weekend house in Mount Tremper, outside Woodstock, New York. Select fresh, small steamers or canned clams, allowing at least 8 ounces of fresh clams per person. Cook them on top of the chard, as the recipe directs. This is a "Sunday Best" recipe.

COOKING TIME: 10 minutes
YIELD: 2 to 4 servings

6	ounces dry, uncooked chile-flavored linguine for 2 servings
1 1/2	Tablespoons extra-virgin olive oil, preferably Spanish
4	large cloves garlic, chopped
1	bunch red Swiss chard, romaine lettuce, or spinach, well-rinsed
2	(6 1/2-ounce) cans chopped clams in clam juice, undrained
1/4	cup white wine, preferably dry, such as Chardonnay
1	teaspoon or more crushed red pequin quebrado chile

Bring a large pot of salted water to a boil and cook the pasta according to package directions. In a 9- to 12-inch heavy skillet over medium-high heat, warm the oil. Add the garlic and cook briefly, stirring, then add the chard. Stir and cook for 2 to 3 minutes. Add the clams and wine and cook for 3 to 4 minutes more. Drain the pasta and serve the sauce over the hot pasta.

PER SERVING (1/4 recipe): Calories 427, Protein 23 g, Carbohydrates 63 g, Fiber 7 g, Fat 8 g, Saturated Fat 1 g, Cholesterol 33 mg, Sodium 302 mg

Green Chile Cilantro Pesto

Green chiles and cilantro are naturals together in this vegetarian delight. Cilantro tames the spicy "edge" of the chiles and adds a fresh taste. The pesto is good with the addition of pan-seared scallops, shrimp, or cubed chicken breast. This is a "Sunday Best" recipe.

COOKING TIME: 10 minutes
YIELD: 4 servings

   10 ounces dry, uncooked angel hair pasta, vermicelli, or thin spaghetti
  1/4 cup low-sodium vegetable stock
    1 cup parched (instructions on page xvii), peeled, and seeds removed chopped green chiles
    2 Tablespoons piñons
  1/4 cup coarsely chopped cilantro, including some stems
  1/2 cup grated Romano cheese
  1/4 cup extra-virgin olive oil, preferably Spanish
       Salt, if needed
       Crushed northern New Mexican red caribe chile for garnish, optional

Bring a large pot of salted water to a boil and cook the pasta according to package directions.

To make the pesto, in a blender or food processor on medium speed, blend the vegetable stock, green chiles, piñons, cilantro, and cheese until just ground. Open the insert in the lid and pour the oil in a fine stream. Continue blending until all the oil has been incorporated.

Taste the pesto and add salt, if desired. Drain the pasta and divide among the plates. Top each serving with the pesto. Garnish with the caribe chile, if desired.

PER SERVING: Calories 427, Protein 24 g, Carbohydrates 63 g, Fiber 7 g, Fat 8 g, Saturated Fat 1 g, Cholesterol 33 mg, Sodium 302 mg

Chipotle Salsa Tossed with Pasta

The original chipotle salsa was probably pico de gallo, the popular salsa for serving over fajitas. With the popularity of chipotles, many salsas featuring these chiles are now available commercially, and several of them are quite good.

COOKING TIME: 10 to 12 minutes
YIELD: 2 large or 4 small servings

10	ounces dry, uncooked pasta, any shape
2	cups chipotle salsa or 1 3/4 cups tomato-based salsa with 1/4 cup minced reconstituted chipotles (see page 59)
1/2	cup Mediterranean-type olives, sliced in strips, pits removed
1/4	pound bacon, fried, drained, and crumbled
1/4	cup coarsely chopped cilantro
	Grated Romano or Parmesan cheese for garnish, optional

Bring a large pot of salted water to a boil and cook the pasta according to package directions. In a small pan combine the salsa, olives, bacon, and cilantro. Simmer for 5 minutes to blend the flavors. When the pasta is done, drain and divide among the plates. Top each with the salsa. Sprinkle with the cheese, if desired.

VEGETARIAN VARIATION: Omit the bacon.

PER SERVING (1/4 recipe): Calories 382, Protein 18 g, Carbohydrates 65 g, Fiber 8 g, Fat 6 g, Saturated Fat 1 g, Cholesterol 16 mg, Sodium 923 mg (Analyzed with Canadian bacon.)
PER SERVING (1/4 recipe): Calories 383, Protein 14 g, Carbohydrates 64 g, Fiber 8 g, Fat 8 g, Saturated Fat 2 g, Cholesterol 8 mg, Sodium 634 mg (Analyzed with regular bacon.)

Pasta Scramble

Make this any time you want a light meal that is quick to make. You can add as many vegetables or cooked meats to the mixture as you have on hand. This is a "Sunday Best" recipe.

COOKING TIME: 5 minutes
YIELD: 2 servings

1	teaspoon extra-virgin olive oil, preferably Spanish
4	scallions, thinly sliced (discarding coarse green tops)
2	cloves garlic, minced
2	cups cooked pasta
4	large eggs, beaten
1	fresh jalapeño chile, minced
1/3	cup grated Parmesan or Romano cheese
	Crushed or ground red chile for garnish, optional

In a large skillet over medium-high heat, warm the oil. Add the scallions, garlic, and pasta. Cook, stirring, until the pasta is lightly browned on some of the edges. Reduce the heat to low and add the beaten eggs, jalapeño, and cheese. Stir the mixture as it cooks. When the eggs are done to your liking, serve. Sprinkle with the red chile, if desired.

PER SERVING: Calories 415, Protein 24 g, Carbohydrates 37 g, Fiber 2 g, Fat 18 g, Saturated Fat 7 g, Cholesterol 441 mg, Sodium 327 mg (Analyzed with Romano cheese.)
PER SERVING: Calories 360, Protein 26 g, Carbohydrates 37 g, Fiber 2 g, Fat 12 g, Saturated Fat 4 g, Cholesterol 19 mg, Sodium 414 mg (Analyzed with egg substitute.)

*A "Sunday Best" recipe with more than five ingredients but fewer than ten.

POLLO . . . POULTRY,
QUICK TO PLEASE

Chicken takes well to the bright, clear flavors of chiles, cilantro, and Southwestern spices. Chicken breast in particular is the darling of low-fat, quick cooking. To save cost, whenever you see chicken breasts on sale, buy extra. To freeze them, just trim the excess fat, if any, then rinse, pat dry, and place on a wax paper–lined baking sheet. When they are frozen solid, place in a plastic bag, label, and seal. To thaw, place them on a plate, cover with plastic wrap, and place in the refrigerator. Quick thawing is best done in a sealed plastic bag in warm water.

I have included some traditional favorites, such as the chilaquiles, a must-try (page 66), Soft Chicken Tacos (page 70), and yummy Sweetheart Barbecued Chicken (page 71), which is flavored with chile, honey, and balsamic vinegar and is easy to prepare.

The subtle flavor of turkey seems to require a few more than five ingredients, but the dishes are still quick to prepare. My husband, Gordon, particularly liked Turkey Chili with a Margarita Splash (recipe on page 76).

Chicken Chilaquiles con Salsa

The origins of this recipe are authentically Mayan. In a weeklong, full-participation course I developed for my New Mexican cooking school in Cozumel, we studied the similarities and differences of Mayan and New Mexican dishes. This popular breakfast dish recipe is from a chef at the Melia Mayan Hotel, where we conducted the class.

COOKING TIME: 15 minutes
YIELD: 4 servings

>   Nonstick oil spray
> 8   corn tortillas*
> 1   pound chicken breasts, approximately 2 breasts, cooked**
> 1   cup tomato-based salsa
> 1   cup chicken broth
> 1/4 cup crumbled Asadero or feta or shredded Jack cheese
> 1/4 cup low- or nonfat sour cream, plus 4 teaspoons for garnish, optional

Preheat the oven to 350°F (180°C). Spray a 2-quart baking dish—8 x 8-inch, 9-inch round, or 10-inch oblong—with nonstick oil spray. Cut the tortillas into sixths and place in the dish in an even layer. Shred the chicken and arrange over the tortillas. Top with the salsa, broth, and cheese. Add 4 teaspoons sour cream, if desired, and bake until bubbly and heated through. Serve hot. Garnish each serving with a dollop of sour cream, if desired.

* Leftover fried corn tortillas or corn tortilla chips can be used, but the fat content will be a great deal higher.

** If you have no leftover cooked chicken breast, poach chicken breasts, covered with chicken broth, in the microwave oven for 2 to 3 minutes. Or cook on top of the stove in a saucepan for 6 to 8 minutes.

PER SERVING: Calories 348, Protein 41 g, Carbohydrates 28 g, Fiber 4 g, Fat 8 g, Saturated Fat 3 g, Cholesterol 106 mg, Sodium 408 mg (Analyzed with commercial salsa, Asadero cheese, and no optional ingredients.)

Chicken with Rice Skillet

Chicken and rice are good together and can be prepared in many ways. The classic is Arroz con Pollo, a tomato-based dish with a Spanish flair. I prefer a version that has a chicken stock or light cream base. Most any salad or green vegetable would nicely complete this dinner.

COOKING TIME: 18 to 20 minutes
YIELD: 4 servings

> 2 cups uncooked quick-cooking long-grain rice
> 2 whole boneless, skinless chicken breasts or 6 to 8 boneless, skinless thighs
> 1 to 2 (4-ounce) cans chopped green chiles
> 1 (14 1/2-ounce) can chicken broth
> 1 (5-ounce can) evaporated milk or 1/3 cup evaporated skim milk

Place the rice in a heavy, deep, seasoned skillet, then add the chicken, chiles, broth, and milk. Cook, covered, over high heat until the sauce simmers, then reduce the heat to low and cook for 15 minutes. Uncover and check for doneness. Taste and adjust the flavoring.* Serve hot.

* For added color and flavor, add a 4-ounce jar of pimiento strips.

PER SERVING: Calories 542, Protein 39 g, Carbohydrates 84 g, Fiber 3 g, Fat 4 g, Saturated Fat 1 g, Cholesterol 77 mg, Sodium 825 mg (Analyzed with chicken breast, low-sodium broth, and evaporated skim milk.)

Garlic- and Chipotle-Sauced Chicken Breast

Chipotles have a strong, smoky quality due to the fact that they are smoked, ripe jalapeño chiles. A mild-mannered side dish such as rice, mashed or baked potatoes, or pasta makes a good "bed" to absorb the yummy juices.

COOKING TIME: 8 to 10 minutes
YIELD: 4 servings

1 to 1 1/2	teaspoons ground pure chipotles or 2 or 3 dried chipotle chiles, reconstituted*
1	teaspoon cider vinegar
4	large cloves garlic
1/4	cup ground pure mild red chile
1/2	teaspoon ground cumin
4	boneless, skinless chicken breast halves, trimmed of all fat and sinew
	Cooked rice, potatoes, or pasta for accompaniment

If reconstituting the dried pods, pour the juice from cooking the chipotles into a measuring cup and add enough water to make 1/2 cup liquid. Otherwise, pour 1/2 cup water into a blender and add the chipotle powder or stewed chipotle chiles, vinegar, garlic, ground chile, and cumin. Process until smooth. Transfer the chile mixture to a nonreactive bowl and add the chicken breasts, coating each side.

Heat the grill, stovetop grill, or a well-seasoned skillet to medium-high. Cook the chicken (reserving the marinade) for about 4 minutes per side. Cook the marinade in a saucepan for 3 to 4 minutes. Serve over rice or potatoes, spooning on sauce.

* To soften the chipotle chiles, see page 59. Or use 1 to 1 1/2 teaspoons chipotle powder instead of the reconstituted dried pods.

PER SERVING: Calories 167, Protein 28 g, Carbohydrates 5 g, Fiber 2 g, Fat 4 g, Saturated Fat 1 g, Cholesterol 73 mg, Sodium 73 mg

Quick Cilantro Chicken

Cilantro, when properly handled, is a fresh, flavored accent that tames spicy, hot chile flavors. Always remember to only coarsely chop it; never mince. Mincing causes the cilantro to develop a strong, disagreeable odor. Serve this chicken with Herbed Quick-Baked Potato Wedges (recipe on page 104).

COOKING TIME: 6 to 8 minutes
YIELD: 4 servings

1 1/2 pounds boneless, skinless chicken breast tenders or 4 chicken breast halves
8 cloves garlic, minced
2 Tablespoons extra-virgin olive oil, preferably Spanish
1 1/2 teaspoons Dijon mustard
1/4 cup coarsely chopped cilantro
4 lime wedges for garnish, optional

Rinse the chicken breasts and pat dry. In a small bowl combine the garlic, oil, mustard, and cilantro.* Generously coat the chicken pieces.

Preheat the grill, stovetop grill, or a heavy, seasoned skillet. Add the chicken and cook for 3 to 4 minutes per side, turning only once, when the chicken starts to curl at the edges and feels firm to the touch. Serve garnished with a lime wedge, if desired.

* For a spicy version, add 1 teaspoon crushed pequin quebrado, a hot red chile, to the coating mix.

PER SERVING: Calories 253 g, Protein 35 g, Carbohydrates 2 g, Fiber 0 g, Fat 11 g, Saturated Fat 2 g, Cholesterol 94 mg, Sodium 108 mg

Soft Chicken Tacos

I prefer soft tacos because they complement the flavors of the filling more than crisp tacos do. The ultimate tacos are prepared with freshly made corn tortillas, which is how tacos were originally prepared. They began as children's snacks when their mothers began cooking meals in which tortillas were a staple.

COOKING TIME: 6 to 8 minutes
YIELD: 4 servings

- 1 pound boneless, skinless chicken breasts
- 1 Tablespoon Basic Rub (recipe on page 173)
- 8 corn tortillas
   Finely shredded romaine lettuce
- 1/2 cup Tomatillo Salsa (recipe on page 160) or purchased salsa

Rinse the chicken and pat dry. Pound with a tenderizer mallet or the flat side of a heavy knife. Rub each side of the breast with the rub. Wrap the tortillas in aluminum foil and warm them for 5 to 10 minutes or until warm in a 350°F (180°C) oven, or just before serving, heat them in a plastic bag for 1 minute in the microwave oven or heat them individually on a hot comal (cast iron griddle).

Preheat a stovetop grill or a griddle. Cook the chicken for 3 to 4 minutes per side, turning only once. (It will be ready to turn when it starts to curl on the edges and feels firm.) Slice into strips and place on half of each tortilla. Top with the lettuce and salsa, roll up, and serve.

PER SERVING: Calories 255, Protein 27 g, Carbohydrates 28 g, Fiber 4 g, Fat 4 g, Saturated Fat 1 g, Cholesterol 63 mg, Sodium 570 mg

Sweetheart Barbecued Chicken

The tangy, honey-edged spiciness of these barbecued chicken thighs is wonderful. While the grill is heating, place some sweet potato rounds, cut 1/2 inch thick, on it. To complete the meal, steam green beans splashed with orange juice in the microwave oven.

COOKING TIME: 8 to 10 minutes
YIELD: 4 servings

    8   chicken thighs, skinned and deboned, fat removed
    1   teaspoon ground pure hot chile or to taste
    4   cloves garlic, minced
    2   Tablespoons honey
    2   Tablespoons balsamic vinegar
        Fresh spinach for garnish, optional

Rinse the chicken and pat dry. In a small bowl combine the chile, garlic, honey, and vinegar. Spoon or brush the mixture evenly over the chicken. Set aside for at least 10 minutes.

Preheat the grill, stovetop grill, or a heavy, seasoned skillet to medium-high. Add the chicken and cook for 4 to 5 minutes, then turn and grill the other side. The chicken is done when it is firm to the touch when pressed or a meat thermometer registers 185°F (85°C). Serve on a bed of fresh spinach, if desired.

PER SERVING: Calories 442, Protein 59 g, Carbohydrates 28 g, Fiber 4 g, Fat 10 g, Saturated Fat 3 g, Cholesterol 154 mg, Sodium 450 mg

Turkey Enchiladas

Using ground turkey to make enchiladas is much faster than stewing a chicken, hence this little twist on my favorite Green Chile Chicken Enchiladas. Black beans go well with these. Simmer with a Tablespoon or two of salsa for a delicious flavor. Serve these enchiladas flat, New Mexico style. This is a "Sunday Best" recipe.

COOKING TIME: 20 minutes
YIELD: 4 servings

SAUCE

1 pound ground turkey breast
1 1/2 cups chicken broth (1 [14 1/2-ounce] can)
1 (4-ounce) can chopped green chiles or 1/2 cup fresh or frozen parched (instructions on page xvii), peeled, and chopped green chiles (4 to 6 chiles)
1/4 teaspoon freshly ground cumin, optional

ENCHILADAS

8 corn tortillas
1 small onion, chopped
1/2 cup shredded Cheddar and Monterey Jack cheeses
Romaine lettuce, rinsed and coarsely chopped, for garnish
1 large tomato, cut into 16 wedges, for garnish

To make the sauce, place the turkey in a cold, heavy skillet. Place over medium-low heat and stir regularly to break up the lumps. After cooking a minute or two, increase the heat to medium and cook, stirring, for about 5 minutes, or until the meat turns white. Add the broth and stir until the sauce thickens. Reduce the heat to low to keep the sauce warm.

Preheat the oven to 350°F (180°C). Place some of the sauce in the center of 4 ovenproof plates. Top each with a tortilla, then a spoonful of sauce, a sprinkle of onion, and 1 Tablespoon of the cheese.

Repeat with another tortilla on each plate, topping each with one quarter of the remaining sauce, one quarter of the onion, and 1 Tablespoon of the cheese. Place each plate in the oven for about 5 minutes (or the microwave oven for 1 1/2 minutes each), or until the filling bubbles. Garnish each enchilada with lettuce and 4 tomato wedges. Serve hot.*

VARIATION: To the sauce add one or two of the following: 10-ounce package frozen, chopped spinach, 1 (15 1/4-ounce) can whole kernel corn, or 1 (15 1/4-ounce) can black beans.

* The enchiladas can be prepared ahead of time on the plates and allowed to set for up to an hour at room temperature or 3 to 4 hours if refrigerated.

PER SERVING: Calories 341, Protein 39 g, Carbohydrates 31 g, Fiber 4 g, Fat 8 g, Saturated Fat 4 g, Cholesterol 98 mg, Sodium 602 mg

Pollo Rellenos

Relleno in Spanish means "stuffed." These chicken rolls stuffed with green chiles and cheese are delicious. This dish is just made for microwave cooking. Top with the salsa garnish or a prepared salsa, if desired. Serve with your favorite rice pilaf seasoned with lots of freshly ground cumin and a salad of tossed woodland greens with a vinaigrette dressing.

COOKING TIME: 10 to 12 minutes in a microwave oven
YIELD: 4 servings

- 4 boneless, skinless chicken breast halves, trimmed of any fat or sinew*
- 2 Tablespoons low-fat Cheddar cheese
- 2 Tablespoons chopped green chile (canned or frozen)
- 1/4 cup skim milk or buttermilk
- 1/2 cup cornflake crumbs**
-    Salsa Garnish (recipe follows)

Rinse the chicken and pat dry. Pound with a tenderizer mallet or the flat side of a heavy knife. Lay the chicken breasts out flat and divide the cheese and chiles among them. Roll the chicken and fasten with toothpicks or skewers, tucking in the sides to hold the cheese mixture. Dip in the milk to coat uniformly, then dip into the cornflake crumbs. Place in a microwave-safe baking dish, cover with wax paper, and cook on high for 10 to 12 minutes. Prepare the Salsa Garnish, if using. Spoon a ribbon of salsa over each serving.

Salsa Garnish

- 1/2 cup chopped tomato
- 1/2 cup chopped onion
- 1/2 cup chopped green chiles

In a bowl combine the tomato, onion, and chiles and mix well.

* Boneless, skinless thighs can be substituted, if preferred.
** Cheese-cracker crumbs can be substituted for the cornflake crumbs, but they contain more fat.

PER SERVING: Calories 205, Protein 29 g, Carbohydrates 13 g, Fiber 1 g, Fat 3 g, Saturated Fat 1 g, Cholesterol 74 mg, Sodium 242 mg

Grilled Turkey Tenders

Grilled turkey is especially good with the spicy onion rings. Served on a bed of mixed salad greens—mesclun or baby greens are the best—with a loaf of crusty peasant bread, this dish is a delicious lunch or a light dinner. This is a "Sunday Best" recipe.

COOKING TIME: 10 to 12 minutes
YIELD: 4 servings

1	large red onion
1/2	cup cider vinegar
1	teaspoon crushed red pequin quebrado chile
1 1/4 to 1 1/2	pounds turkey tenders, trimmed of any fat or sinew
2	teaspoons extra-virgin olive oil, preferably Spanish
6	cups mixed salad greens

Slice the onion into thin rings. Preheat a large, heavy, seasoned frying pan over medium-high heat. Place the onions in the dry pan and cook, stirring and turning the rings for a minute or two, until they are light tan on the edges and somewhat softened. Remove to a bowl, then add the vinegar and chile and stir to mix. Cover to keep warm.

Meanwhile, rinse the turkey tenders and pat dry. Pound with a tenderizer to about 1/2 inch thick. Slice in lengths so they will fit easily in the frying pan. Lightly and evenly oil the outside of each tender. Grill them for 4 1/2 minutes per side in a seasoned pan or on a grill, or until the flesh is no longer pink and the turkey is firm to the touch.

Transfer to a cutting board and slice into 1/2-inch-wide strips. Arrange a bed of lettuce on each plate. Top with the turkey strips and warm onions and serve.

PER SERVING: Calories 252, Protein 46 g, Carbohydrates 7 g, Fiber 2 g, Fat 4 g, Saturated Fat 1 g, Cholesterol 123 mg, Sodium 100 mg

Chicken Breasts Baked in Salsa

Salsa is much more than just a good dip for chips. Serve this chicken over pasta or rice.

COOKING TIME: 16 to 20 minutes
YIELD: 4 servings

 4 **boneless, skinless chicken breast halves (4 to 6 ounces each), trimmed of any fat or sinew**
    Few drops of vegetable oil or oil spray
 1 **cup salsa**
 1 **small onion, sliced into thin rings**
    Cooked rice or pasta for accompaniment
    Southwestern-flavored goat cheese (see page 11) or nonfat sour cream for garnish, optional

Rinse the chicken and pat dry. Warm the oil in a heavy, seasoned skillet.* Add the chicken and cook for 3 to 4 minutes, until the chicken is lightly browned. Turn and brown the other side for about 3 minutes or until frim to the touch.

Reduce the heat to low, pour the salsa over the chicken, and scatter with the onion rings. Cover and allow to steam for 4 to 6 minutes, until the chicken is fork-tender. Serve on rice or pasta, spooning the sauce over the chicken. Top with the goat cheese, if desired.

* To cook the chicken in the microwave oven, place the chicken in a baking dish, sear it for 1 1/2 minutes per side, top with the salsa and onion rings, and cover tightly. Cook for 7 to 10 minutes, until tender.

PER SERVING: Calories 175, Protein 28 g, Carbohydrates 6 g, Fiber 1 g, Fat 4 g, Saturated Fat 0 g, Cholesterol 73 mg, Sodium 133 mg (Analyzed with 1/2 teaspoon oil and Hot New Mexican Table Salsa.)

Turkey Chili with a Margarita Splash

Leftover roast turkey makes a marvelous curtain call when served in this chili. If you don't have any leftover turkey or roast turkey from a deli, quickly sauté ground turkey for about 2 minutes in the microwave oven or a bit longer on the stovetop. You can vary this chili in endless ways—for instance, by using navy or cannellini beans or red chiles instead of the green. Serve with warm corn or flour tortillas for a complete light meal. This is a "Sunday Best" recipe.

COOKING TIME: 15 minutes
YIELD: 4 servings

1	medium onion, chopped
1	(14 1/2-ounce) can low-sodium, low-fat chicken broth
1	(4-ounce) can chopped green chiles
1	(15 1/4-ounce) can black beans
2	cups chopped, cooked turkey or 1 pound ground skinless turkey breast or chicken, sautéed*
1 1/2	teaspoons ground cumin
1	lime, juiced, for garnish, optional
	Jigger of tequila for garnish, optional

Place the onions in a cold, heavy saucepan. Sauté over medium-high heat for about 2 minutes, or until the onion starts to brown on the edges. Reduce the heat to medium-low and cook, stirring, for about 5 minutes, or until the onion darkens or caramelizes in its own juices. Immediately add the broth, chiles, beans, turkey, and cumin. Simmer for 8 to 10 minutes. Serve with about a teaspoon or so each of freshly squeezed lime juice and tequila, if desired.

* To sauté the ground turkey in the microwave oven, break up the lumps, place in a microwavable bowl, and cover. Cook on high for 2 to 3 minutes. Stir and cook longer if needed. To cook on the stovetop, place the turkey (as above) in a cold, well-seasoned skillet and sauté over medium heat for 3 to 5 minutes.

PER SERVING: Calories 241, Protein 29 g, Carbohydrates 21 g, Fiber 7 g, Fat 5 g, Saturated Fat 2 g, Cholesterol 55 mg, Sodium 763 mg (Analyzed without the tequila or lime juice.)

SEAFOOD SOUTHWEST—SI, SI!

Seafood in the Southwest is now commonplace. Not so long ago, fresh fish—except for stream and lake fish such as trout, bass, and the like—were rare because most of the Southwest has no coastline. Mexico, of course, is blessed with generous amounts of fresh fish and seafood.

Many of my recipes were inspired by my childhood and numerous trips to Mexico. Other recipes were developed to take advantage of the beautiful harmony between chiles, salsa, and seafood.

Red snapper is abundant in the Southwest and Mexico. If you cannot find them, substitute any firm-fleshed fish, such as halibut.

The concept of this book—to prepare meals quickly and easily—is especially natural with fish and seafood because they cook quickly and take on spicy flavors readily. Fresh chiles accented with lime are a wonderful addition to any fish. Placing the fish mixture in a freshly made or warmed corn tortilla produces a soft taco.

*A "Sunday Best" recipe with more than five ingredients but fewer than ten.

Guaymas Shrimp

Succulent and sweet, these spicy shrimp are delicious, especially when served with Mexicali Rice Pilaf (recipe on page 108).

COOKING TIME: 6 to 10 minutes
YIELD: 4 servings

1	Tablespoon extra-virgin olive oil, preferably Spanish
4	cloves garlic, minced
1	pound uncooked shrimp, peeled and deveined
1	teaspoon crushed red caribe chile, plus more for garnish
1 1/2	teaspoons freshly squeezed lime juice (1/2 lime)
	Cooked rice for accompaniment, optional
	Lime wedges for garnish, optional

Warm the olive oil in a heavy, well-seasoned skillet. Add the garlic and stir, then add the shrimp. Cook for 3 to 5 minutes; turn the shrimp and cook until they become pink and lose their glossy appearance. Sprinkle the shrimp with the chile and lime juice and lightly toss together. Arrange on 4 serving plates. If desired, circle with rice and garnish with caribe chile and lime wedges.

NOTE: To cook in the microwave oven, in a glass pie plate or similar cooking utensil, stir together the oil and garlic. Add the shrimp, cover with waxed paper or plastic wrap, and cook on full power for 1 minute. Stir, re-cover, and cook for another 30 seconds, or until the shrimp are barely pink and no longer shiny.

PER SERVING: Calories 118, Protein 18 g, Carbohydrates 1 g, Fiber 0 g, Fat 4 g, Saturated Fat 1 g, Cholesterol 161 mg, Sodium 187 mg

Peppered Scallop Fajitas

Tucked into a fresh flour tortilla (or corn, if you prefer), these scallops make a quick and wonderful light meal.

COOKING TIME: 6 to 8 minutes
YIELD: 4 servings

- 4 cloves garlic, minced
- 2 Tablespoons freshly squeezed lime juice (1 lime)
- 1 pound bay scallops
- 1 medium red bell pepper, cut into 1/2-inch dice
- 4 flour tortillas
  Pico de Gallo (recipe on page 168)

In a large bowl combine the garlic and lime juice. Add the scallops and stir to mix well. In a well-seasoned skillet over medium-high heat, cook the red peppers, stirring occasionally, until they start to wilt and turn brown around the edges. Add the scallop mixture and cook, stirring, for 2 to 3 minutes, until the scallops are white and just cooked. Warm the tortillas for 20 seconds, covered, in the microwave oven or briefly over a burner. Top with the scallop mixture and serve with the pico de gallo.

PER SERVING: Calories 309, Protein 16 g, Carbohydrates 45 g, Fiber 3 g, Fat 7 g, Saturated Fat 1 g, Cholesterol 18 mg, Sodium 578 mg (Analyzed without the Pico de Gallo.)

Pan-Seared Tuna Steaks on Spinach a la Baja

Fresh tuna steaks are so good that they should be only subtly enhanced. This tease with orange and garlic is just perfect. Most people agree that tuna should be cooked only to the rare to medium stage to preserve the moist, fresh flavor. For this dish to be at its best, the tuna must be cut about an inch thick—no less. Wilt the fresh spinach in the same pan. For a wonderful, quick meal, special enough for company, serve the tuna with beans and rice, either a pilaf mix or your favorite rice. Heat a cup of canned black beans, stir in the rice, and top with coarsely chopped cilantro, flat-leaf parsley, chives, or scallions. This is a "Sunday Best" recipe.

COOKING TIME: 6 to 8 minutes
YIELD: 2 servings

- 1 orange
- 2 cloves garlic, minced
- 1 Tablespoon vegetable oil or oil spray, optional
- 2 (5- to 6-ounce) fresh tuna steaks, cut 1 inch thick
- 1 (10-ounce) package fresh spinach, rinsed
- 3 Tablespoons balsamic vinegar

Using a zester or a grater on the fine setting, zest the very outside (orange part only) of the orange. Squeeze the juice into a small bowl.

In a shallow, nonreactive bowl, combine the orange zest, juice, and garlic. Add the tuna and press into the liquid; turn the tuna and press the other side into the marinade. Let stand at room temperature at least 10 minutes and up to 2 hours.

About 10 minutes before serving time, heat a heavy, well-seasoned skillet until hot over medium-high heat. (Water sprinkles should dance on the surface when it is hot enough.) Remove the tuna from the marinade (reserve the marinade) and cook for 4 minutes, then turn and cook for about 3 minutes. Keep warm.

Add the spinach to the skillet, drizzle with the reserved marinade, and cover. Steam for 3 to 5 minutes, until the spinach is just wilted. Add the vinegar and toss. Arrange on warm serving plates and top with the tuna.

PER SERVING: Calories 259, Protein 38 g, Carbohydrates 16 g, Fiber 4 g, Fat 8 g, Saturated Fat 2 g, Cholesterol 56 mg, Sodium 168 mg

Seared Salmon with Mango Salsa

Salmon is wonderful simply seared in a well-seasoned skillet. Lacking one, you can use vegetable oil in a skillet to prevent scorching and enhance browning.

COOKING TIME: 6 to 10 minutes
YIELD: 4 servings

 1/2 teaspoon salt
 1 Tablespoon vegetable oil, optional
 1 1/2 pounds fresh salmon fillet, skinned and cut into 4 (3-inch-square) pieces, about 1/2 inch thick
 1 1/2 cups Mango Salsa (recipe on page 163)

Sprinkle salt in a heavy, seasoned skillet and place over medium-high heat until hot. (A sprinkle of water will dance on the bottom of the pan when it is hot.) If a seasoned or nonstick pan is not available, add the oil to the pan.

Meanwhile, rinse the salmon and pat dry with a paper towel. Sauté the salmon for 3 to 5 minutes per side, until crisp and brown on the outside and still moist and bright pink on the inside. Serve with the salsa.

PER SERVING: Calories 256, Protein 34 g, Carbohydrates 2 g, Fiber 0 g, Fat 11 g, Saturated Fat 2 g, Cholesterol 96 mg, Sodium 368 mg (Analyzed without the vegetable oil.)

Chile-Seared Salmon with Sweet Pear Piña Salsa

A dusting or rub of chile on salmon adds a wonderful flavor. Pan searing or grilling works equally well. If the weather is not conducive to grilling or if you are in a hurry, pan searing is ideal.

COOKING TIME: 6 to 10 minutes
YIELD: 2 servings

- 1 Tablespoon ground mild red chile
- 1 teaspoon sugar
- 1/2 teaspoon salt, plus more for seasoning skillet
- 3/4 pound fresh salmon fillet, deboned, if necessary
- 1 Tablespoon vegetable oil, optional
- 1 cup Sweet Pear Piña Salsa (about 1/2 recipe) (recipe on page 164)

In a small bowl combine the chile, sugar, and salt. Cut the salmon into 2 pieces. Rinse, then pat dry with a paper towel. Rub the chile mixture evenly over the salmon.

Sprinkle salt in a heavy, seasoned skillet (or an unseasoned skillet to which you have added the oil). Place over medium-high heat until hot. (A sprinkle of water will dance in the bottom of the pan when it is hot.) Sauté the salmon for 3 to 5 minutes per side, until crisp and brown on the outside and still moist and bright pink on the inside. Serve on a pool of salsa.

PER SERVING: Calories 388, Protein 35 g, Carbohydrates 34 g, Fiber 4 g, Fat 12 g, Saturated Fat 2 g, Cholesterol 96 mg, Sodium 661 mg

Chilled Salmon with Cilantro Salsa

Sometimes, especially in the hot summer, chilled, poached salmon is just the ticket. You can use this poached salmon for lots of meals, such as salads, tacos, omelets, and dips. You can enhance the poaching liquid by adding white wine, lemon juice, and pickling mix or fish boil,* but salmon poached only in water until just done is simple yet good, especially when time is short.

COOKING TIME: 15 minutes
YIELD: 4 servings

    4 (6- to 8-ounce) salmon steaks
1 3/4 cups Cilantro Salsa (recipe on page 165)

Heat 3 inches of water in a 5-quart Dutch oven that is not more than 4 to 5 inches deep. When the water is just at a simmer, add the fish in a single layer. Cover, reduce the heat, and steam for about 15 minutes, or until the flesh flakes yet is still moist. Remove from the heat and chill. Serve with the salsa.

* If you wish to add white wine, add 1 cup to 4 cups water. The juice of half a lemon and 1 teaspoon fish boil or pickling mix may also be added to the poaching liquid.

VARIATION: Cucumber Salsa (recipe on page 161) is also good on this salmon.

PER SERVING: Calories 268, Protein 35 g, Carbohydrates 5 g, Fiber 1 g, Fat 11 g, Saturated Fat 2 g, Cholesterol 96 mg, Sodium 78 mg (Analyzed with 6 ounces of salmon.)

Blue Corn–Crusted Red Snapper
with Chipotle Cantaloupe Salsa

The blue corn crust creates a flavorful crunch around the moist snapper. The perfect finish is Chipotle Cantaloupe Salsa.

COOKING TIME: 10 to 12 minutes
YIELD: 4 servings

8	small red snapper fillets (about 1 1/2 pounds)
1/3	cup blue corn flour or white or yellow cornmeal
2 to 3	Tablespoons vegetable oil
	Chipotle Cantaloupe Salsa (recipe on page 162)

Rinse the snapper fillets and pat dry. Dust with the corn flour. In a large, heavy skillet, heat the oil. When water dances in the skillet, add the floured fillets and sauté for 5 to 6 minutes, until lightly browned. Turn and sauté the other side. Serve napped with the salsa.

PER SERVING: Calories 254, Protein 25 g, Carbohydrates 17 g, Fiber 2 g, Fat 9 g, Saturated Fat 1 g, Cholesterol 42 mg, Sodium 58 mg

Snapper Sauced in Salsa

Red snapper is served many ways down Mexico way. This version is a quick and easy adaptation of the famous Vera Cruz–style red snapper. Serve with your favorite rice pilaf or steamed rice. A mixed green or fresh spinach salad tartly dressed and a hard, crusty bread would be good accompaniments.

COOKING TIME: 5 to 8 minutes
YIELD: 4 servings

8	small red snapper fillets (about 1 1/2 pounds)
2/3	cup tomato-based salsa
1/2	cup dry white wine
	Mexicali Rice Pilaf (recipe on page 108) or Herbed Quick-Baked Potato Wedges (recipe on page 104) for accompaniment
4	sprigs cilantro for garnish, optional
4	lime wedges for garnish, optional

Rinse the snapper fillets and pat dry. Place in a heavy, well-seasoned cold sauté pan. Spread the salsa evenly over the fillets. Pour the wine into the pan, being careful not to disturb the salsa on the fish. Cover and steam for 5 to 8 minutes, until the fish flakes easily. Garnish with the cilantro and lime wedges, if desired. Serve with the rice or potatoes.

PER SERVING: Calories 149, Protein 24 g, Carbohydrates 4 g, Fiber 1 g, Fat 10 g, Saturated Fat 0 g, Cholesterol 42 mg, Sodium 100 mg

Crumb-Coated Halibut with Tomatillo Salsa

Halibut steaks are succulent and generally available. The steaks are juicier and come from a better-quality fish than the fillets; avoid the smaller fillets altogether.

COOKING TIME: 8 to 10 minutes
YIELD: 4 servings

    4 (1-inch-thick) halibut fillets
    1 lemon, halved lengthwise
  1/2 cup bread crumbs, preferably fresh
    2 teaspoons ground pure hot red chile
    2 teaspoons extra-virgin olive oil, preferably Spanish
    1 cup Tomatillo Salsa (recipe on page 160) for garnish, optional

Preheat the oven to 400°F (200°C). Rinse the fish and pat dry, then place on an aluminum foil–covered baking sheet. Top each fillet with a squeeze of lemon juice from half the lemon.

In a small bowl mix the bread crumbs and chile together, then sprinkle on the top, bottom, and sides of each fillet. Drizzle the oil over the top of each. Place in the oven and bake until the fish flakes easily (approximately 8 to 10 minutes) when pierced with a fork. Cut the remaining half lemon lengthwise into quarters. Serve the fish napped with the salsa and a lemon wedge.

PER SERVING: Calories 217, Protein 38 g, Carbohydrates 4 g, Fiber 0 g, Fat 6 g, Saturated Fat 0 g, Cholesterol 57 mg, Sodium 127 mg (Analyzed with 6 ounces halibut steak and no Tomatillo Salsa.)

Tamale-Style Catfish

Especially in the summertime, catfish or other firm-fleshed white fish such as orange roughy or tilapia is delicious baked with fresh corn. For a summery treat, serve with your favorite coleslaw.

COOKING TIME: 12 to 15 minutes
YIELD: 4 servings

  4 ears of fresh corn, or 1 (15 1/4-ounce) can whole kernel corn, or 1 (10-ounce) package frozen corn kernels
  1 (4-ounce) can chopped green chiles
1/2 cup chopped scallions (3 or 4)
  1 lime, halved lengthwise
  4 (4- to 6-ounce) catfish fillets
  1 teaspoon crushed red caribe chile for garnish, optional

Preheat the oven to 400°F (200°C). If using fresh corn, carefully peel back the husk. You will use it for baking the fish. Cut the ear of corn off the stem just above the end of the cob, leaving the husk intact. Set the husk aside. Cut the corn off the cob and combine in a bowl with the green chiles, scallions, and the juice of half the lime.

Rinse the fish and pat dry. Place one fillet inside each of the corn husks. Top each with one-fourth of the corn mixture and overlap the husks together. (If fresh corn is not available, place the fish in an oiled baking dish. Top with the corn mixture and cover.)

Bake for 12 to 15 minutes, until the fish flakes easily. Cut the remaining half lime lengthwise into 4 wedges. Serve the fish in the husk with a lime wedge on top. (Or spoon the corn out of the baking dish and place on each plate. Top with the fish and a lime wedge.)

PER SERVING: Calories 252, Protein 22 g, Carbohydrates 23 g, Fiber 3 g, Fat 11 g, Saturated Fat 2 g, Cholesterol 54 mg, Sodium 83 mg

SOUP'S ON!

When I was a child I visited my aunt and uncle who lived in Oaxaca, Mexico, and they started every noon meal with *sopa*, or soup. Their wonderful, freshly made soups were often flavored with chiles and were usually broth based.

Borrowing from this taste memory, I developed many of these soups. Corn tortillas are a popular thickener and are ever present. When they simmer and break down after a few moments of cooking, the resulting soup has a marvelous flavor and a texture approaching that of a chowder.

Many of these recipes are flexible, allowing for substituting your favorite or on-hand ingredients. An example is Salsa Snapper Soup (recipe on page 91), which can be made with any fish or shellfish or chicken.

Try fresh corn or wheat-flour tortillas as an accompaniment to these soups instead of crackers or bread. Corn tortillas are especially healthy for you. If the tortillas are not fresh, cut them into thin strips (which I call shoestrings), bake them until crisp, and scatter them over any bowl of soup. (Follow the recipe for preparing them on page 6 for Tortilla Toasts.)

*A "Sunday Best" recipe with more than five ingredients but fewer than ten.

Salsa Snapper Soup

Homemade salsa is best, but you can use a favorite commercial variety. Shellfish such as shrimp or scallops, or even chicken, can be substituted for the fish. This soup is hearty enough for a light dinner. If you'd like something more, serve warmed fresh corn tortillas and a simple salad.

COOKING TIME: 10 to 20 minutes, depending on the rice used
YIELD: 2 large or 4 small servings

3 (14 1/2-ounce) cans chicken broth, preferably low sodium
1/2 cup quick-cooking white rice or pasta shells
1 (15 1/4-ounce) can corn kernels or 1 (12-ounce) package frozen corn kernels
1 pound firm-fleshed fish, such as red snapper, cut into 1-inch chunks
1 cup tomato-based or tomatillo-type salsa (canned, fresh, or frozen)
1 lime, cut into wedges for garnish, optional

In a saucepan heat the chicken broth until it simmers, then add the rice. Bring to a boil, reduce the heat, and simmer until almost done. Add the corn, fish, and salsa. Simmer, covered, just a few minutes until the fish is just done and white in color. Serve hot with lime wedges, if desired.

PER SERVING (1/4 recipe): Calories 284, Protein 24 g, Carbohydrates 42 g, Fiber 4 g, Fat 4 g, Saturated Fat 2 g, Cholesterol 34 mg, Sodium 347 mg (Analyzed with rice and frozen corn.)

Quick Green Chile Stew

Green chile stew is a popular dish in New Mexico, especially around the time of the green chile harvest. Green chiles become bountiful from August through mid-October, and most New Mexicans freeze at least a forty-pound bag per family. More green chiles are consumed in New Mexico than anywhere in the world. This stew is made in many ways, with most cooks agreeing that green chiles, pork, tomatoes, onion, and garlic are the essential ingredients. Serve the stew with warm, buttered flour tortillas for a satisfying lunch or light dinner.

COOKING TIME: 20 minutes
YIELD: 2 large servings

- 1 pound lean loin or shoulder pork chops, cut into 1/2-inch dice
- 1/2 cup chopped onion (1/2 medium onion)
- 2 cloves garlic, minced
- 1 (14 1/2-ounce) can peeled tomatoes, diced
- 1 (7-ounce) can chopped green chiles
  Salt, optional
- 2 wheat-flour tortillas

In a heavy, 3-quart pot, arrange the diced pork in a uniform layer. Cook over medium-high heat until the pork begins to sizzle. Stir to turn each piece, then continue cooking for 5 to 6 minutes, until the pork is lightly browned. Add the onion, garlic, tomatoes, and chiles.

Cover, reduce the heat to low, and simmer for about 10 minutes, stirring occasionally. Taste and add salt if desired. Warm the tortillas (see page 2), butter them, and serve with the stew.

PER SERVING (1/2 recipe): Calories 362, Protein 42 g, Carbohydrates 27 g, Fiber 4 g, Fat 10 g, Saturated Fat 4 g, Cholesterol 100 mg, Sodium 433 mg

Speedy Chili

My favorite chili is the Bowl o' Red, a true Texas-type chili (see *Jane Butel's Tex-Mex Cookbook* by Turner Publishing), which is made without beans or tomatoes. Freshly ground red chiles coupled with garlic, onion, and cumin flavor that dish. About three hours of simmering are required to develop the flavors. For a speedier preparation, try this chili, which is quite respectable when you consider the short simmering time. Chili improves with age. Making it a day or so ahead and refrigerating or freezing it brings out a rich flavor. With its abundance of red chiles, the world's best antioxidant, this dish can be frozen for at least a year. I always serve red chili with Fixin's 'n Mixin's (as detailed in the Super Bowl Party menu on page 202). This is a "Sunday Best" recipe.

PREPARATION TIME: 20 minutes
YIELD: 4 servings

- 1 pound ground chuck (80 percent lean)
- 1/2 cup chopped onion, cut into 1/2-inch dice
- 2 cloves garlic, minced
- 3 Tablespoons freshly ground pure mild red New Mexican chile
- 1 (14 1/2-ounce) can water-packed stewed tomatoes, diced
- 1 teaspoon freshly ground cumin or to taste
- 1/2 teaspoon salt or to taste
- 1 (15-ounce) can pinto beans, optional
  Fixin's 'n Mixin's (see page 202) for garnish

Crumble the meat into a heavy, 5-quart Dutch oven–type pot. Sauté over medium heat until the pink color disappears. Tilt the pot and spoon out any visible fat. Add the onion and garlic to the pot and continue simmering for 3 to 5 minutes, until the onion becomes soft and clear.

Remove the pot from the heat and stir in the chile, tomatoes, cumin, and salt. Add the beans, if using.* Return to the heat and simmer for another 10 to 15 minutes. Taste and adjust the seasonings. If time allows, refrigerate for a day or two so the flavors can develop. If not, serve immediately with the Fixin's 'n Mixin's.

* Many Southwestern chili buffs prefer to cook the chili and beans separately, then serve the beans on the bottom of the bowl, topped with the chili and Fixin's 'n Mixin's.

PER SERVING: Calories 261, Protein 21 g, Carbohydrates 11 g, Fiber 3 g, Fat 15 g, Saturated Fat 6 g, Cholesterol 72 mg, Sodium 592 mg (Analyzed without beans and with 80 percent lean ground beef.)
PER SERVING: Calories 352, Protein 27 g, Carbohydrates 28 g, Fiber 8 g, Fat 16 g, Saturated Fat 6 g, Cholesterol 72 mg, Sodium 904 mg (Analyzed with beans and 80 percent lean ground beef.)
PER SERVING: Calories 244, Protein 25 g, Carbohydrates 11 g, Fiber 3 g, Fat 11 g, Saturated Fat 4 g, Cholesterol 41 mg, Sodium 607 mg (Analyzed without beans and with 91 percent lean ground beef.)

Chile-Sparked Sweet Potato Soup

This hearty soup is wonderful for lunch served with just a crunch of baked tortilla toasts. Serve the soup with a sandwich for a light dinner.

COOKING TIME: 12 minutes in a microwave oven, 20 minutes in a conventional oven
YIELD: 4 servings

- 2 medium sweet potatoes, peeled and cut into 1/2-inch dice
- 4 scallions, thinly sliced (1 Tablespoon sliced tops reserved for garnish)
- 1 cup evaporated skim milk
- 1 Tablespoon ground pure hot red chile or to taste, divided
  Few grates of fresh nutmeg
  Baked tortilla toasts (recipe on page 6) for garnish, optional

Place the potatoes, scallions, and 1 cup water in a 2-quart glass or microwavable bowl. Cover with plastic wrap or waxed paper and microwave on full power for 10 minutes.*

Transfer the potato mixture to a food processor. Add the milk and 2 teaspoons of the chile and process until pureed. Stir in the nutmeg. Return to the 2-quart container and microwave for about 2 minutes, or until hot. Serve each bowl garnished with the reserved chile, scallions, and tortilla shoestrings, if desired.

* To cook conventionally, place the sweet potatoes, 1 cup water, and scallions in a heavy, medium saucepan, cover, and simmer for about 15 minutes, or until fork-tender. Puree as above.

PER SERVING: Calories 142, Protein 6 g, Carbohydrates 28 g, Fiber 3 g, Fat 1 g, Saturated Fat 0 g, Cholesterol 2 mg, Sodium 86 mg

Chipotle-Teased Black Bean Pumpkin Soup

The smoky heat of the chipotles adds a spark to the hearty goodness of black beans. Pumpkin or any winter squash is a wonderful complement to black beans. I make spicy black bean soup and butternut squash soup and puree each separately. To serve, I pour them simultaneously into each bowl. This one soup captures these twin flavors quickly and easily. This is a "Sunday Best" recipe.

COOKING TIME: 20 minutes
YIELD: 2 large or 4 small servings

> 1 (15-ounce) can black beans, undrained
> 1 (14 1/2-ounce) can chicken broth, preferably low-sodium
> 1 cup chopped onion (1 large onion)
> 1 dried chipotle chile, reconstituted (see page 59) and minced, or 1/2 teaspoon chipotle powder
> 1 (15-ounce) can pumpkin
> 1 to 2 teaspoons ground cumin
> Salt to taste, optional

Optional Garnishes

> 1 lime, cut into wedges
> 2 Tablespoons sour cream
> 2 to 4 sprigs cilantro

In a heavy, 3-quart saucepan, combine the beans, broth, onion, chile, and pumpkin. Bring to a simmer and cook for about 10 minutes, or until the onion softens. Transfer the mixture to a blender or food processor and whirl until thick and smooth. Return to the pan and add 1 teaspoon of the cumin; taste to determine if you desire the remaining cumin. Add salt, if desired. Serve in bowls. If desired, garnish with a squeeze of lime, a dollop of sour cream, and a sprig of cilantro.

PER SERVING (1/4 recipe): Calories 143, Protein 9 g, Carbohydrates 26 g, Fiber 10 g, Fat 2 g, Saturated Fat 1 g, Cholesterol 2 mg, Sodium 381 mg

Pumpkin Pinto Bisque

Squash have long been popular in Southwestern cooking. The Pueblo Indians of New Mexico harvested bountiful crops of all kinds of squash, even the wild calabacitas that grow anywhere there is water. Pinto beans are prevalent too, making for a perfect marriage in this bisque. Serve it with warm corn tortillas for a quick and easy light meal.

COOKING TIME: 15 to 20 minutes
YIELD: 4 servings

　　1　cup diced onion (1 large onion), 4 teaspoons reserved for garnish
　　1　(15 1/2-ounce) can pinto beans, undrained
　　1　(15-ounce) can pumpkin
　1/2　teaspoon salt or to taste
　　1　(12-ounce) can evaporated skim milk
　　1　Tablespoon ground pure hot red chile or to taste, plus more for garnish

Place the onion in a heavy, nonstick pan with a close-fitting cover. Cook over medium heat for 3 to 4 minutes, until the onion becomes clear. Add the beans, pumpkin, salt, milk, and chile. Reduce the heat to low and simmer for 10 to 15 minutes, until the flavors blend. Serve in large bowls topped with a sprinkle of chile and the reserved onion.

PER SERVING: Calories 221, Protein 14 g, Carbohydrates 40 g, Fiber 9 g, Fat 2 g, Cholesterol 3 mg, Sodium 732 mg

Fall Harvest Soup

Any winter squash is good in this vegetarian soup, even a leftover jack-o'-lantern that you have baked. I prefer baked squash to canned; however, when time is short, canned pumpkin is an acceptable substitute. It combines beautifully with the sage in this streamlined version. This is a "Sunday Best" recipe.

COOKING TIME: 20 minutes
YIELD: 2 large or 4 small servings

   1 (15-ounce) can pumpkin
6 to 8 fresh sage leaves or 1/2 teaspoon ground dried sage, 2 to 4 leaves reserved for garnish
  1/2 teaspoon salt
       Several grinds of black pepper
   2 teaspoons ground pure hot red New Mexican chile
   1 onion, chopped
   2 cloves garlic, minced
   1 (5-ounce) can evaporated skim milk

In a heavy, 3-quart saucepan, combine the pumpkin, sage, salt, pepper, chile, onion, and garlic. Rinse out the pumpkin can with 1 cup water and add to the pan. Bring to a simmer and cook for 15 minutes.

Transfer the mixture to a food processor or blender and process until smooth. Add the milk, return the mixture to the pan, and cook for 3 to 5 minutes to blend the flavors. Taste and adjust the seasonings. Serve in warm soup bowls garnished with the sage leaves or a dash of ground sage.

PER SERVING (1/4 recipe): Calories 84, Protein 5 g, Carbohydrates 17 g, Fiber 4 g, Fat 1 g, Saturated Fat 0 g, Cholesterol 1 mg, Sodium 344 mg

Southwestern Chicken Vegetable Soup

Made from grilled chicken, perhaps left over from a previous grilled dinner, this soup is quick to prepare. Summer calabacitas or zucchini give it a fresh flavor.

COOKING TIME: 15 minutes
YIELD: 2 large or 4 small servings

1 (14 1/2-ounce) can chicken broth, preferably low-sodium
1 cup cubed grilled chicken, cut into 1/2 inch dice
1 large tomato, cut into 1-inch chunks
1 small zucchini, thinly sliced
2 large cloves garlic, minced
  About 1/2 teaspoon crushed caribe chile for garnish, optional

In a heavy, 3-quart saucepan, combine the broth, chicken, tomato, zucchini, and garlic. Simmer for about 15 minutes. Serve warm. For a colorful garnish, dust with the caribe chile.

PER SERVING (1/4 recipe): Calories 86, Protein 13 g, Carbohydrates 4 g, Fiber 1 g, Fat 3 g, Saturated Fat 1 g, Cholesterol 32 mg, Sodium 78 mg

Green Chile Corn Chowder

This soup is best made with fresh corn grilled without the husk. Canned or frozen corn kernels are good substitutes.

COOKING TIME: 15 minutes
YIELD: 2 large or 4 small servings

  1 (15 1/4-ounce) can whole kernel corn or 2 medium ears corn grilled and kernels removed
  1 (14 1/2-ounce) can chicken broth, preferably low-sodium
1/2 cup diced onion
  1 (4-ounce) can diced green chiles
  1 tomato (canned or fresh), diced
     Corn chips for garnish, optional

In a heavy, 3-quart saucepan, combine the corn, broth, onion, chiles, and tomato. Simmer uncovered for 15 minutes. Taste and adjust the seasonings. Serve in warm bowls with a few corn chips on top of each if desired.

PER SERVING (1/4 recipe): Calories 99, Protein 4 g, Carbohydrates 22 g, Fiber 3 g, Fat 2 g, Saturated Fat 1 g, Cholesterol 2 mg, Sodium 613 mg (Analyzed with fresh tomato.)

Chicken Tortilla Chowder

The hearty, full flavor and creamy consistency of this chicken soup taste like work, but this dish is actually fast and easy to make. Cutting the chicken breast is the most time-consuming part of the recipe. This is a versatile dish that you can vary in many ways. Instead of chicken breasts, you could use leftover roast chicken or turkey, or firm-fleshed fish or shellfish with fish stock, or roast beef or ground chuck with beef stock.

COOKING TIME: 10 to 12 minutes
YIELD: 2 servings

1 (14 1/2-ounce) can chicken broth, preferably low-sodium, with water added to make 2 cups
2 white or yellow corn tortillas, broken up
1 pound chicken breasts, trimmed and cut into 1-inch cubes (for a lighter version, use only 1/2 pound chicken)
3 scallions, thinly sliced, reserve some for garnish
1 1/2 Tablespoons minced pickled jalapeño chiles with juice

OPTIONAL GARNISHES

Cilantro leaves
Crushed red caribe chiles
Lime wedges

Place the chicken broth and water in a 3-quart saucepan over medium heat. Add the tortillas and chicken. Cover, reduce the heat to low, and simmer, stirring, for 5 to 6 minutes. Add the scallions and jalapeños with juice. Stir to combine well. Simmer for about another 5 minutes. Serve garnished with the reserved scallion and, if desired, the cilantro, chiles, and lime to squeeze on the chowder.

PER SERVING: Calories 326, Protein 50 g, Carbohydrates 14 g, Fiber 2 g, Fat 8 g, Saturated Fat 2 g, Cholesterol 130 mg, Sodium 338 mg

MEAL COMPLEMENTS

The side dishes served at the typical "touristy" Southwestern or Mexican restaurant in the United States are predictable—almost always pinto beans and rice in various forms.

There are many alternatives. All of these meal complements are quick to make; most have five ingredients or fewer. Some of the dishes are based on vegetables rarely seen in Southwestern cooking, such as kale, but they are flavored with Southwestern seasonings.

Potatoes are a member of the nightshade family, as are chiles, and were probably cultivated in northern Peru at about the same time. Potatoes are very compatible with chiles. I hope you will enjoy combining the two.

I've developed some rice combinations that I think you'll like. Try the Salsa Verde Rice (recipe on page 109) or the Green Chile Cheese Rice (recipe on page 110).

I had lots of fun developing chile combinations with greens, squash, and the like. Try the Mexican-Style Grilled Corn (recipe on page 120); it is a treat with any of the toppings. The Quick Corn Custard with Chiles (recipe on page 122) is wonderful too.

*A "Sunday Best" recipe with more than five ingredients but fewer than ten.

Chipotle and Roasted Garlic Mashed Potatoes

The rich flavors of chipotle chiles laced with roasted garlic are wonderful in mashed potatoes. Infusing the potatoes with butter makes for a rich flavor. This is a "Sunday Best" recipe.

COOKING TIME: 15 minutes
YIELD: 8 servings

- 3/4 teaspoon salt
- 4 pounds russet, golden, or baking potatoes, peeled and quartered
- 1 1/2 Tablespoons unsalted butter
- 1/2 head garlic, roasted*
- 3/4 cup milk (skim for lowest fat or evaporated skim for a richer flavor)
- 2 dried chipotle chiles, reconstituted (see page 59) and minced, or 1 teaspoon chipotle powder

Bring about an inch of salted water to a boil. Add the potatoes, cover, and cook for about 15 minutes, or until the potatoes are tender. Drain well, then add the butter. Cover and let stand while preparing the garlic.

Slice off the root end of the garlic. With the blunt edge of a knife, squeeze the garlic from the husk; mince and set aside. Warm the milk for about 30 seconds. Mash the potatoes using a masher, slowly adding milk and mashing until the potatoes are fluffy. Fold in the minced chiles and garlic. Serve hot.

* To roast garlic, lightly oil the head, then cover with foil or place in a garlic baker (lots of garlic can be done at once). Bake in the oven at 400°F (200°C) for 20 to 30 minutes or until soft to the touch when pressed.

PER SERVING: Calories 204, Protein 4 g, Carbohydrates 42 g, Fiber 4 g, Fat 2 g, Saturated Fat 1 g, Cholesterol 6 mg, Sodium 241 mg (Analyzed with skim milk.)

Herbed, Quick-Baked Potato Wedges

These are delicious with most any meal or even as a snack. They are best when made with starchy, fresh, high-quality potatoes. The fresh herbs can be varied to suit what you have available. Favorites are rosemary, Italian parsley, thyme, marjoram, or sage.

COOKING TIME: 15 to 20 minutes
YIELD: 4 servings

> 4 medium potatoes (any kind), unpeeled
> 1 Tablespoon extra-virgin olive oil, preferably Spanish
> 2 Tablespoons finely minced mixed fresh herbs or 2 teaspoons crushed dried herbs
> 1/2 teaspoon salt or to taste
> Several grinds black pepper

Preheat the oven to 450°F (230°C). Slice the potatoes lengthwise, then cut into 3/4-inch-wide wedges. Place on a baking sheet and drizzle with the oil. In a small bowl combine the herbs, salt, and pepper, then sprinkle on the potatoes. Bake for 15 to 20 minutes (stirring after about 7 minutes for even baking), until the potatoes are tender and somewhat browned on the tips.

VARIATION: Sweet potatoes can be substituted.

PER SERVING: Calories 163, Protein 3 g, Carbohydrates 31 g, Fiber 3 g, Fat 4 g, Saturated Fat 0 g, Cholesterol 0 mg, Sodium 10 mg

Papas con Chile (Potatoes with Chile)

Chile rub, which is popular to use on meats, is also good on potatoes and other starchy vegetables.

COOKING TIME: 15 minutes
YIELD: 4 servings

4 medium to large baking potatoes (about 2 pounds)
2 Tablespoons Basic Rub (recipe on page 173)

Preheat the oven to 450°F (230°C). Scrub the potatoes, then cut into 1/2-inch-thick slices. Sprinkle the rub uniformly on one side of each slice and rub in. Place rub side up in a single layer on a baking sheet. Bake for about 15 minutes or until the potatoes are soft in the center. Serve hot.

PER SERVING: Calories 141, Protein 3 g, Carbohydrates 33 g, Fiber 4 g, Fat 0 g, Saturated Fat 0 g, Cholesterol 0 mg, Sodium 514 mg (Note: Using less rub will reduce sodium.)

Presto Potato Salad

This flavorful potato salad is made with virtually no fat. Although I love to infuse the potatoes with butter for potato salad, the combination of flavors here works well without it. You can serve this immediately or refrigerate it for an hour or more, allowing the flavors to blend. This is a "Sunday Best" recipe.

COOKING TIME: 15 minutes
YIELD: 4 servings

- 2 pounds potatoes, preferably a baking type such as russet
- 3/4 cup nonfat mayonnaise
- 1/3 cup nonfat sour cream
- 2 scallions, minced
- 1 large stalk celery, finely chopped
- 1 Tablespoon cider vinegar
- 1/2 teaspoon salt
- 2 teaspoons crushed red caribe chile

Place an inch of water in a 3-quart saucepan with a close-fitting cover and bring to a boil. Peel and cut the potatoes into 1-inch dice. Place in the boiling water, cover, reduce the heat to medium-low, and cook for about 15 minutes or until fork-tender.

In a bowl large enough to hold the potato salad, combine the mayonnaise, sour cream, scallions, celery, vinegar, salt, and chile. When the potatoes are done, drain them immediately and add to the bowl. Stir to combine.

PER SERVING: Calories 232, Protein 5 g, Carbohydrates 52 g, Fiber 4 g, Fat 0 g, Saturated Fat 0 g, Cholesterol 2 mg, Sodium 645 mg

Sweet Potatoes with Chile and Herbs

Quick-baked sweet potato rounds tossed in balsamic vinegar, chiles, and herbs are perfect with any pork or poultry dish. They are easy to make and, to me, are much better than the candied, gooey sweet potatoes popular during the holidays.

COOKING TIME: 15 to 20 minutes
YIELD: 4 servings

2   medium to large sweet potatoes (about 1 pound)
2   Tablespoons balsamic vinegar
1   Tablespoon Basic Rub (recipe on page 173)
1   Tablespoon minced fresh herbs, such as sage or thyme, or 1 teaspoon ground dried herbs

Preheat the grill or preheat the oven to 450°F (230°C). Scrub the potatoes but leave unpeeled. Slice in 1/2-inch rounds. Place the rounds on a baking sheet and sprinkle with the vinegar, followed by the rub and herbs. Bake for 15 to 20 minutes, until the potatoes are fork-tender. Serve hot.

PER SERVING: Calories 81, Protein 1 g, Carbohydrates 19 g, Fiber 2 g, Fat 0 g, Cholesterol 0 mg, Sodium 513 mg

Mexicali Rice Pilaf

This salsa-flavored rice is perfect with seafood or poultry entrées. When made with vegetable stock, it is a good vegetarian dish and is flavorful enough to stand on its own as an entrée. This is a "Sunday Best" recipe.

COOKING TIME: 16 or more minutes
YIELD: 4 servings

- 2 cups chicken or vegetable broth or stock
- 1 cup uncooked long-grain rice
- 1/2 cup parched (instructions on page xvii), peeled, and chopped green chiles (2 to 4 chiles) or 1 (4-ounce) can green chiles
- 1/2 cup chopped Spanish onion
- 1/2 cup chopped tomato
- 1 clove garlic, minced
  About 1 teaspoon salt, if needed

Bring the stock to a boil in a 3-quart saucepan with a close-fitting cover. Add the rice, chiles, onion, tomato, and garlic. Taste to determine the need for salt. Reduce the heat, cover, and simmer for 15 minutes or until all the liquid is absorbed. Taste and adjust the seasonings. Serve hot.

PER SERVING: Calories 219, Protein 6 g, Carbohydrates 45 g, Fiber 2 g, Fat 2 g, Saturated Fat 1 g, Cholesterol 3 mg, Sodium 60 mg

Salsa Verde Rice

Sometimes known as green rice, this attractive and fresh-tasting rice is particularly good with poultry or seafood. When made with vegetable stock, this is a delightful vegetarian rice dish.

COOKING TIME: 15 to 20 minutes
YIELD: 4 servings

- 2 cups chicken or vegetable stock
- 1 cup uncooked long-grain rice
  About 1 teaspoon salt, if needed
- 1 cup Tomatillo Salsa (recipe on page 160)
- 1 garlic clove, minced
  Cilantro leaves for garnish, optional

Bring the stock to a boil in a 3-quart saucepan with a close-fitting cover. Add the rice. Taste to determine the need for salt. Reduce the heat, cover, and simmer for 15 minutes or until all the liquid is absorbed. Stir in the salsa and garlic. Taste and adjust the seasonings. Garnish each serving with a cilantro leaf, if desired.

PER SERVING: Calories 212, Protein 6 g, Carbohydrates 44 g, Fiber 2 g, Fat 2 g, Saturated Fat 1 g, Cholesterol 3 mg, Sodium 58 mg

Green Chile Cheese Rice

Golden Cheddar or mixed, shredded Cheddar and Monterey Jack cheeses are good stirred into fluffy rice with an overtone of green chiles. This side dish is delicious with any entrée.

COOKING TIME: 15 to 20 minutes
YIELD: 4 servings

- 2 cups chicken or vegetable broth or stock
- 1 cup uncooked long-grain rice
  About 1 teaspoon salt, if needed
- 1/2 cup parched (instructions on page xvii), peeled, and chopped green chiles (2 to 4 chiles) or 1 (4-ounce) can green chiles
- 1/2 cup shredded Cheddar cheese or mixed Monterey Jack and Cheddar, or more to taste
- 1/2 cup nonfat sour cream or to taste

Bring the stock to a boil in a 3-quart saucepan with a close-fitting cover. Add the rice. Reduce the heat, cover, and simmer for 15 minutes, or until the rice is soft and fluffy and all the liquid is absorbed.

Remove from the heat and stir in the chiles, cheese, and sour cream. Cover for 3 to 5 minutes for the cheese to melt and the flavors to blend. Taste and adjust seasoning. Add more cheese, if desired. Serve hot.

PER SERVING: Calories 297, Protein 11 g, Carbohydrates 49 g, Fiber 1 g, Fat 6 g, Saturated Fat 4 g, Cholesterol 20 mg, Sodium 170 mg (Analyzed with Cheddar cheese.)

Snappy Beans 'n Rice

Combining beans and rice almost makes a light meal in itself.

COOKING TIME: 2 to 5 minutes
YIELD: 4 servings

2   cups cooked rice*
1   (16-ounce) can pinto or black beans, drained, or 2 cups cooked
1/2 cup parched (instructions on page xvii), peeled, and chopped green chiles (2 to 4 chiles) or
    1 (4-ounce) can green chiles
2   Tablespoons ground pure hot red chile
2   teaspoons freshly ground cumin
    Stock (any kind), if needed

In a large bowl combine the rice, beans, chopped chiles, ground chile, and cumin. Cover with plastic wrap and microwave on high for 2 minutes. Stir, taste, and adjust the seasonings. Serve hot.

* To cook rice, follow the package instructions, or for 2 cups cooked rice, bring 1 1/2 cups water to a boil with 1/2 teaspoon salt in a 3-quart saucepan with a close-fitting cover. When boiling, add 2/3 cup regular long- or medium-grain rice. Stir and reduce heat, then cover when it comes to a simmer. Cook for 15 minutes without removing the cover. Check for doneness and fluff with a fork.

NOTE: To cook this meal conventionally in a heavy, 3-quart saucepan, combine 1/4 cup water or stock (any kind), the rice, beans, chopped chiles, ground chile, and cumin. Stir and cook, uncovered, for 3 to 5 minutes on medium-low heat.

PER SERVING: Calories 243, Protein 10 g, Carbohydrates 49 g, Fiber 9 g, Fat 2 g, Saturated Fat 0 g, Cholesterol 0 mg, Sodium 245 mg

Very Quick Refritos (Refried Beans)

The secret to flavorful refried beans is "tingeing" the garlic, or sautéing it until it just begins to turn tan. Even canned beans come to life with the toasted garlic.

COOKING TIME: 6 to 8 minutes for refried beans, 12 to 15 minutes for whole beans
YIELD: 4 servings

- 2 teaspoons unsalted butter, bacon drippings, or lard
- 2 cloves garlic, minced
- 1 (16-ounce) can refried beans or whole pinto beans without fat
  Stock (chicken or vegetable), if needed

In a heavy, seasoned skillet over medium-high heat, melt the butter. Add the garlic, stirring constantly. When the garlic begins to turn tan, add the beans. Stir if refried; mash with a masher if whole. If the beans become dry, add stock or water. Serve hot to accompany a Southwestern meal, or use as an ingredient in other dishes.

PER SERVING: Calories 126, Protein 6 g, Carbohydrates 18 g, Fiber 6 g, Fat 3 g, Saturated Fat 2 g, Cholesterol 14 mg, Sodium 359 mg (Analyzed with butter.)

Chilied Cheesy Grits

Grits are totally Southern yet are popular in Texas, which is dead center between the Deep South and the West. Grits became popular in the West because so many Southerners kept moving farther and farther west and took their grits with them. These are good as a side dish with most any meat or with eggs for breakfast.

You can also use the grits as a base for seared vegetables. Just slice the seared vegetables into thin strips and serve over the hot grits. You may wish to omit the cheese from the grits when serving them this way.

COOKING TIME: 5 to 7 minutes
YIELD: 4 servings

- 1/2 cup quick-cooking grits
-   2 cloves garlic, minced
- 1/2 cup parched (instructions on page xvii) peeled, and chopped green chiles (2 to 4 chiles) or 1 (4-ounce) can green chiles
- 1/2 cup shredded Cheddar cheese, preferably low-fat

Bring 2 cups water to a boil, then slowly add the grits, stirring constantly. Reduce the heat to low, cover, and cook for 5 to 7 minutes, until all the water is absorbed. Add the garlic, chiles, and cheese. Cook, stirring, for about 2 minutes, or until the cheese melts. Serve immediately.

VARIATIONS: Make red chile grits by substituting 2 Tablespoons ground pure red chiles for the green chiles. Stir in the chiles until the grits are uniformly pinkish red.

PER SERVING: Calories 111, Protein 6 g, Carbohydrates 19 g, Fiber 1 g, Fat 1 g, Saturated Fat 1 g, Cholesterol 3 mg, Sodium 88 mg (Analyzed with low-fat Cheddar cheese.)

Spicy Sesame Spinach

This quick and easy spinach is a perfect low-fat side dish. It can be enhanced with other vegetables or tossed with pan-seared meats for a light meal.

COOKING TIME: 6 to 7 minutes
YIELD: 2 servings

1	Tablespoon sesame seeds
3	cups loosely packed fresh spinach, well-rinsed
1 1/2	teaspoons red wine vinegar or to taste
1/2	teaspoon crushed red pequin quebrado flakes or to taste

In a heavy skillet with a lid, toast the sesame seeds for 2 to 3 minutes over medium heat, stirring frequently. Add the spinach, cover, reduce heat to low, and cook for about 5 minutes, or until wilted. Season with the vinegar and chile, adding more if desired, and serve.

PER SERVING: Calories 34, Protein 2 g, Carbohydrates 3 g, Fiber 2 g, Fat 2 g, Saturated Fat 0 g, Cholesterol 0 mg, Sodium 38 mg

Orange Caribe Steamed Cabbage

Cabbage prepared this way is wonderful as a side dish with most any meat or seafood. We had it first with salmon; however, you can serve it just as well with poultry, pork, or beef.

PREPARATION TIME: 5 to 7 minutes
YIELD: 4 servings

- 1 Tablespoon vegetable oil
- 4 cups finely shredded cabbage (1/2 head)
- 1/2 teaspoon salt or to taste
  Few grinds of black pepper
  Zest of 1 orange, chopped
- 1 teaspoon sesame oil or to taste
- 2 Tablespoons freshly squeezed orange juice

Warm the vegetable oil in a sauté pan over medium-high heat. Add the cabbage and sprinkle with the salt and pepper. Toss and cook, stirring, for 3 to 5 minutes, until the cabbage is slightly wilted. Add the zest, sesame oil, and orange juice; cook for another 2 to 3 minutes. Taste and adjust the seasonings. Serve immediately.

PER SERVING: Calories 62, Protein 1 g, Carbohydrates 5 g, Fiber 2 g, Fat 5 g, Saturated Fat 1 g, Cholesterol 0 mg, Sodium 303 mg

Shredded Chard or Kale

Thinly sliced big-leaf greens quickly wilted and laced with garlic-infused olive oil are wonderful with most any chile-laden dish.

COOKING TIME: 3 to 5 minutes
YIELD: 4 servings

1	bunch Swiss chard or kale (about 12 ounces), well-rinsed
1 1/2	teaspoons extra-virgin olive oil, preferably Spanish
3	cloves garlic, finely minced
	Sprinkle of crushed northern New Mexican red caribe chile or squeeze of lime or lemon for garnish, optional

Rinse the greens and pat dry. Cut into about 1/4-inch-thick slices by rolling up the leaves tightly, then thinly slicing them. In a heavy, deep skillet on medium-high heat, cook the oil and garlic until the oil is sizzling. Add the greens and cook, stirring, until they are slightly wilted. Serve immediately with the chile or lime, if desired.

PER SERVING: Calories 34, Protein 2 g, Carbohydrates 4 g, Fiber 1 g, Fat 2 g, Saturated Fat 0 g, Cholesterol 0 mg, Sodium 182 mg

Stovetop-Grilled Veggies

Grilling brings out the natural flavors in vegetables and is a wonderful way to make them appealing. You can vary the vegetables according to what you have on hand and to complement the other foods you are serving. This is a "Sunday Best" recipe.

COOKING TIME: 5 to 8 minutes
YIELD: 4 servings

- 1 eggplant
- 1 teaspoon salt or to taste
- 8 scallions or 1 medium onion, sliced 1/4 inch thick
- 1 red bell pepper, cut into 1/2-inch-wide strips
- 2 small zucchini, sliced into 1/4-inch-thick strips
  Dressing (recipe follows)

About 30 minutes before you plan to cook the vegetables, prepare the eggplant. (You can also prepare it hours ahead or even up to 15 minutes ahead.) Using a meat fork, cut through the skin of the eggplant to a depth of about 1/8 inch. Slice into rounds a scant 1/2 inch thick. Lightly salt each side of each slice, then place the slices on a plate, with a double layer of paper toweling between each layer of slices.

Place wood chips or dried herb stalks in the water pan of a stovetop grill. Add water, following the manufacturer's instructions, then preheat the grill to medium. Or use any type of outdoor or indoor grill.

Pat both sides of the eggplant slices dry. Place on the grill, then add the scallions, red pepper, and zucchini as there is room. Grill the vegetables for 3 to 4 minutes per side. Remove to a platter, keeping all the vegetables of each kind together.

Prepare the dressing. Uniformly sprinkle it over the vegetables and serve at once.

DRESSING

- 2 Tablespoons extra-virgin olive oil, preferably Spanish
  Juice of 1 lime
- 2 cloves garlic, minced
- 1 teaspoon ground pure hot red chile, optional

In a small bowl combine the oil, lime juice, garlic, and chile, if using.

VARIATION: Toss the grilled vegetables together and serve over Chilied Cheesy Grits (recipe on page 113).

PER SERVING: Calories 118, Protein 2 g, Carbohydrates 13 g, Fiber 4 g, Fat 7 g, Saturated Fat 1 g, Cholesterol 0 mg, Sodium 588 mg (Analyzed with 1 teaspoon salt for the eggplant and 1 medium onion instead of scallions.)

Quick Roasted Winter Squash

Winter vegetables of any kind are delicious when quickly roasted. You can vary the vegetables and herbs to suit your taste.

COOKING TIME: 15 to 18 minutes
YIELD: 4 servings

1 pound acorn, butternut, Hubbard, or other type of firm-fleshed winter squash, unpeeled
1 Tablespoon olive oil, preferably Spanish
2 Tablespoons minced fresh herbs, such as thyme, sage, and rosemary, or 1 1/2 teaspoons dried herbs
1 teaspoon salt, optional

Preheat the oven to 450°F (230°C). Cut the squash into 1/2-inch slices and arrange on a baking sheet. Drizzle with the oil and sprinkle with the herbs. Sprinkle with salt, if desired. Bake until the squash is tender and somewhat blackened on the edges. Serve hot.

VARIATIONS: Sweet potatoes, parsnips, carrots, beets, or turnips can be substituted for the squash. Balsamic or wine vinegar can be used instead of the oil for less fat.

PER SERVING: Calories 70, Protein 1 g, Carbohydrates 10 g, Fiber 3 g, Fat 4 g, Saturated Fat 0 g, Cholesterol 0 mg, Sodium 3 mg (Analyzed without salt.)

Calabacitas

Summer squash are popular in the Southwest. In New Mexico, calabacitas, the wild, round, light-green squash, abound by arroyos, or ditches. A popular substitute is zucchini. Yellow summer squash is also a good substitute. For the best color, combine the two.

COOKING TIME: 7 to 8 minutes
YIELD: 4 servings

4	(6-inch-long) zucchini or yellow summer squash or a combination
1 1/2	teaspoons extra-virgin olive oil, preferably Spanish
3	cloves garlic, minced

Cut the zucchini into diagonal slices 1/4 inch thick. Heat the oil in a heavy, seasoned skillet over medium-high heat. Add the garlic and stir, then add the zucchini. Cook for 3 to 4 minutes, until the zucchini is lightly browned on the edges. Stir or flip the zucchini to brown the other side. Cover and let steam for a couple of minutes. Serve immediately.

VARIATIONS: Popular additions are a diced tomato or two, thinly sliced browned onion, corn cut off the cob, and green chiles.

PER SERVING: Calories 36, Protein 2 g, Carbohydrates 4 g, Fiber 2 g, Fat 2 g, Saturated Fat 0 g, Cholesterol 0 mg, Sodium 4 mg

Mexican-Style Grilled Corn

You can grill corn this way on an outdoor grill, under the broiler, or on a stovetop grill. The various toppings make it fun.

COOKING TIME: 12 to 15 minutes
YIELD: 4 servings

4 large ears fresh, sweet corn

Preheat the cooking surface. Husk the corn and remove the silk. Place the corn on the grill and cook until the kernels, when pierced, are firm and not milky. The outside edges of the kernels should be a bit blackened. Serve with your choice of the toppings below.

PER SERVING: Calories 103, Protein 3 g, Carbohydrates 19 g, Fiber 2 g, Fat 3 g, Saturated Fat 0 g, Cholesterol 0 mg, Sodium 13 mg (Analyzed without toppings.)

Grilled Corn Toppings

FRESH LIME AND CARIBE CHILE

1 lime, cut into wedges
4 teaspoons crushed red caribe chile

Serve lime wedges—2 per person per ear—along with a small bowl of the chile.

PER SERVING: Calories 8, Protein 0 g, Carbohydrates 2 g, Fiber 1 g, Fat 0 g, Saturated Fat 0 g, Cholesterol 0 mg, Sodium 0 mg

NEW MEXICAN HERBS

2 Tablespoons extra-virgin olive oil, preferably Spanish
1/2 teaspoon ground Mexican oregano
1/2 teaspoon ground cumin
1/2 teaspoon crushed pequin quebrado chiles

Before grilling the corn, combine the oil, oregano, cumin, and chiles in a small bowl. Serve with the hot corn. This topping can also be used for dipping bread. It will keep for several days at room temperature.

PER SERVING: Calories 62, Protein 0 g, Carbohydrates 0 g, Fiber 0 g, Fat 7 g, Saturated Fat 1 g, Cholesterol 0 mg, Sodium 1 mg

MEXICAN HOT MAYONNAISE

4 Tablespoons (1/4 cup) mayonnaise
1 small jalapeño chile, minced

In a small bowl combine the mayonnaise and jalapeño. Serve with the hot corn.

PER SERVING: Calories 103, Protein 0 g, Carbohydrates 1 g, Fiber 0 g, Fat 11 g, Saturated Fat 2 g, Cholesterol 10 mg, Sodium 76 mg

Spiced Broccoli Sauté

Broccoli has become a popular vegetable due to its healthy attributes. It goes well with any simply prepared meat in this book. If desired, you can place the broccoli florets in a covered bowl and microwave them for about 2 1/2 minutes or until desired doneness.

COOKING TIME: 5 to 8 minutes
YIELD: 4 servings

2 large heads broccoli
2 Tablespoons olive oil, preferably Spanish
3 cloves garlic
2 Tablespoons crushed caribe chile

Wash the broccoli and cut the florets no more than 1/2 inch thick. Meanwhile, warm the oil in a seasoned, deep skillet over medium-high heat. Stir in the garlic and immediately add the broccoli.

Cook for about 3 minutes, or until the florets are somewhat browned on the edges. Stir to turn over the florets and cook to the desired doneness. Remove from the heat and add the chile. Stir, then remove to a serving bowl or to the plates. Serve immediately.

PER SERVING: Calories 98, Protein 3 g, Carbohydrates 7 g, Fiber 4 g, Fat 7 g, Saturated Fat 1 g, Cholesterol 0 mg, Sodium 29 mg

Quick Corn Custard with Chiles

Green chiles and corn have long been "a pair made in heaven." Their flavors are so compatible that you should try them in a dish such as this as soon as you can.

COOKING TIME: 15 minutes
YIELD: 4 to 6 servings

> 1 (15 1/2-ounce) can cream-style corn
> 1 teaspoon unsalted butter
> 1 large egg, beaten
> 2 corn tortillas, torn into small pieces
> 1/2 cup parched (instructions on page xvii), peeled, and chopped green chiles (2 to 4 chiles) or
>   1 (4-ounce) can green chiles

Preheat the oven to 375°F (190°C). Butter 4 (6-ounce) ramekins or 6 (4-ounce) ramekins. In a blender or food processor, combine the corn, butter, egg, and tortillas. Process until pureed.

Stir in the chiles but do not process. Pour the mixture into the ramekins and place them on a baking sheet. Bake for 15 to 20 minutes, until an inserted knife comes out clean. Serve at once.

PER SERVING (1/6 recipe): Calories 96, Protein 3 g, Carbohydrates 19 g, Fiber 2 g, Fat 2 g, Saturated Fat 1 g, Cholesterol 37 mg, Sodium 240 mg

UNDER WRAPS

Wraps have always been "in" in Southwestern and Mexican food. With tortilla-wrapped favorites such as tacos, enchiladas, burritos, chimichangas, and fajitas, to name just a few, you can easily see that this trend is not new. It's just been a fusion of the always-popular Southwestern dishes and other American favorites.

I tried to trim each recipe so that all would be low fat and healthy too. Remember that you can pare quite a few calories by reaching for corn rather than wheat tortillas. For especially low-fat dishes, try Lettuce Lovers, Chimis (recipe on page 134) and Swiss Chard–Wrapped Salmon (recipe on page 133). Rockefeller Roll-Ups (recipe on page 126) and Texas Veggie Hash Burritos (recipe on page 129) are both vegetarian dishes.

Flavored and whole wheat–flour tortillas can be used whenever desired. They taste good and are attractive when cut at angles and sprinkled with a confetti garnish on the plate.

*A "Sunday Best" recipe with more than five ingredients but fewer than ten.

Speedy Enchiladas

Corn tortillas sparked with spicy red or green chile sauce and rolled with beef or chicken and cheese make for a fast entrée.

PREPARATION TIME: 8 minutes in a microwave oven, 20 minutes in a conventional oven
YIELD: 4 servings

2	cups Basic Red Chile Sauce (recipe on page 156) or Favorite Green Chile Sauce (recipe on page 157)
8	corn tortillas
1 1/2	cups cooked chicken or beef, shredded
3/4	cup coarsely shredded Monterey Jack and/or Cheddar cheese, plus 1/4 cup for garnish
1/2	cup chopped onion (1 small onion)
4	leaves romaine lettuce, sliced into 1-inch-wide ribbons for garnish, optional

Heat the chile sauce for about 2 minutes in the microwave oven or 5 to 6 minutes on top of the range. Keep warm. Heat the tortillas over a burner, on a comal (cast iron griddle), or in a plastic bag in the microwave oven for 1 minute at full power or wrapped in aluminum foil for 5 to 10 minutes in a 400°F (200°C) oven. (Leave the oven on for warming the enchiladas.)

Place the tortillas on 4 microwave-safe or ovenproof plates. Place a spoonful of the chile sauce down the center of each tortilla. Divide the meat among the tortillas. Top with the cheese and onion.

Roll up each tortilla, then place seam side down on the plates. Drizzle with the remaining sauce and sprinkle with the reserved cheese. Place in the microwave oven for a minute each or in the conventional oven for 5 to 8 minutes.

PER SERVING: Calories 409, Protein 29 g, Carbohydrates 38 g, Fiber 7 g, Fat 17 g, Saturated Fat 8 g, Cholesterol 80 mg, Sodium 650 mg

PER SERVING: Calories 364, Protein 30 g, Carbohydrates 38 g, Fiber 7 g, Fat 11 g, Saturated Fat 5 g, Cholesterol 66 mg, Sodium 684 mg (Analyzed with low-fat cheese.)

Rockefeller Roll-Ups

Healthy and lean, yet rich enough to be sinful, these fun-to-make vegetarian wraps are good as a snack or a light meal or cut into small appetizer-sized servings. This is a "Sunday Best" recipe.

PREPARATION TIME: 10 to 15 minutes
YIELD: 4 servings

> 1 (12-ounce) package fresh spinach
> 6 ounces (3/4 cup) nonfat cream cheese or goat cheese, softened
> 1 Tablespoon crushed red caribe chiles, plus 1 Tablespoon for garnish
> 1 (15-ounce) can refried black or pinto beans
> 1/2 cup red or green salsa
> 4 (8-inch) wheat-flour tortillas

Rinse the spinach and spin dry. Chop about a fourth of it into 1/2-inch pieces. Reserve the remaining spinach. In a bowl combine the chopped spinach with the cream cheese and 1 Tablespoon of the chiles. Place the beans in a small bowl, cover with plastic wrap, and warm in the microwave oven for 2 minutes on full power.

To assemble the roll-ups, lay the tortillas on a flat surface. Spread each with one-fourth of the cream cheese mixture and the beans. Place 2 Tablespoons of the salsa down the center of each and roll up. Then arrange the reserved spinach leaves on 4 plates. Place the roll-ups on the plates (or eat them out of hand and reserve the spinach for a later use) and sprinkle with the reserved chiles, scattering them over the plates to create a confetti effect.

PER SERVING: Calories 337, Protein 20 g, Carbohydrates 53 g, Fiber 11 g, Fat 6 g, Saturated Fat 2 g, Cholesterol 12 mg, Sodium 888 mg

Chevre Wrap

I created this wrap for Conrad's restaurant, named for Conrad Hilton, the former owner of the historic landmark hotel La Posada de Albuquerque, where our cooking school was located from 1997 to 2005. This dish has been very popular in the restaurant, and when cutting the wrap into two-inch cuts and slicing each on the diagonal, they create clever-looking little flowers when arranged in foursomes with a piece of tomato in the center of each.

PREPARATION TIME: 3 to 5 minutes
YIELD: 1 large serving or 4 appetizers

- 1 (12-inch) spinach or sun-dried tomato wheat tortilla
- 2 Tablespoons low-fat or nonfat herbed chevre (goat cheese)
- 2 Tablespoons Hot New Mexican Table Salsa (recipe on page 158)
- 1/2 cup loosely packed mesclun salad greens
- 1 Tablespoon Cilantro Pesto (recipe on page 166)

Optional Garnishes

- 1 Tablespoon chopped fresh tomato
- 1 teaspoon roasted piñon nuts
  Tomatillo Salsa (recipe on page 160)

Lay the tortilla flat. Spread with the cheese followed by the salsa, greens, and pesto. Roll tightly. If serving 1 person, cut diagonally into 3 pieces. If serving several, party style, cut as mentioned above. Place vertically on a plate and garnish with the tomato, piñons, and salsa, if desired.

PER SERVING (full recipe): Calories 417, Protein 15 g, Carbohydrates 61 g, Fiber 5 g, Fat 12 g, Saturated Fat 2 g, Cholesterol 4 mg, Sodium 708 mg

Oaxacan Gorditos

Gorditos in Spanish means "stuffed ones." Mexican chorizo is different from the Spanish and Portuguese versions. If it's not available, substitute any spicy sausage or pepperoni.

PREPARATION TIME: 15 minutes
YIELD: 4 servings

1/2	pound chorizo, removed from plastic wrappers and coarsely chopped*
1	(15-ounce) can black beans, drained
1 1/2	teaspoons ground cumin
2	dried chipotle chiles, reconstituted (see page 59), or 1 teaspoon chipotle powder
4	(8-inch) wheat-flour tortillas
	Nonfat sour cream for garnish, optional
	Pico de Gallo (recipe on page 168) or any favorite spicy red salsa for garnish, optional

Place the chorizo in a heavy, nonstick skillet over medium-high heat. Cook for about 2 minutes, then stir and turn. Cook for about another 2 minutes. Drain off all excess fat, placing drained chorizo in a double-paper-towel-lined colander.

Return the drained chorizo to the skillet and add the beans. Cook and stir for about 3 minutes. Add the cumin and chiles. Heat the tortillas one at a time. Roll one quarter of the bean mixture in each, folding the bottom 1 inch up and tucking in the sides. Serve with the sour cream and salsa for dipping, if desired.

* Strict draining of chorizo cuts fat and calories.

PER SERVING: Calories 560, Protein 28 g, Carbohydrates 54 g, Fiber 11 g, Fat 26 g, Saturated Fat 9 g, Cholesterol 50 mg, Sodium 1186 mg (Note: 80 percent of the fat and 60 percent of the sodium is from the chorizo.)

Texas Veggie Hash Burritos

This veggie combo for a wrap includes a favorite of Southwestern cuisine—zucchini. This is a "Sunday Best" recipe.

COOKING TIME: 5 minutes in a microwave oven, 15 minutes conventionally
YIELD: 4 servings

- 2 large baking potatoes, unpeeled and diced
- 2 medium zucchini, unpeeled and diced
- 1 small onion, diced
- 2 cloves garlic, minced
- 1 (4-ounce) can green chiles, undrained, or 1/2 cup parched (instructions on page xvii), peeled, and chopped green chiles
  Salt, if needed
- 4 (10- to 12-inch) flour tortillas or 8 (6-inch) corn tortillas

OPTIONAL GARNISHES

Salsa
Shredded cheese
Sour cream

Place the potatoes, zucchini, onion, and garlic in a 2-quart microwave-safe bowl.* Add 1/2 cup water, cover with a lid, waxed paper, or plastic wrap, and cook in the microwave oven on full power for 5 minutes, or until fork-tender. Stir and add the chiles and their liquid. Taste the vegetable mixture and add salt, if desired.

Heat the tortillas (see page 2). Place the vegetable mixture on each tortilla, leaving a 1-inch margin. Fold the bottom 1 inch up around the filling, then roll up the tortilla. Serve with salsa, cheese, and sour cream, if desired.

* If cooking conventionally, simmer vegetables in an inch of water for 12 to 15 minutes until done. Add drained chiles.

PER SERVING: Calories 332, Protein 9 g, Carbohydrates 63 g, Fiber 5 g, Fat 5 g, Saturated Fat 1 g, Cholesterol 0 mg, Sodium 352 mg (Analyzed with flour tortillas and no optional ingredients.)

Shrimp Salad Burritos

Seafood and rice have always been a popular combination. Add the crunch of your favorite salad greens and spicy salsa and you have a quick, sure winner. For speed's sake, prepare the rice ahead. Cooked rice keeps several days in the refrigerator or in the freezer for up to ninety days.

PREPARATION TIME: 3 minutes
YIELD: 4 servings

4 (10-inch) wheat-flour tortillas or 8 corn tortillas
1 cup cooked white rice or Mexicali Rice Pilaf (recipe on page 108), at room temperature
2 cups mixed lettuces, rinsed and spun dry
3/4 pound cooked bay or baby shrimp, peeled, deveined, and chilled
1/4 cup spicy salsa, plus more for garnish

Warm the tortillas over a burner or on a comal (cast iron griddle) in a plastic bag in the microwave oven for 1 minute, or wrapped in aluminum foil in a 350°F (180°C) oven for about 10 minutes.

Place the tortillas on a flat work surface. Place a 2-inch-wide strip of rice down the center of each tortilla, leaving about a 1 1/2-inch margin at one end. Place the lettuce on top of the rice, then top with the shrimp and salsa. Fold the 1 1/2-inch margin up over the filling, then roll the tortilla. Serve immediately with more salsa.

PER SERVING: Calories 180, Protein 26 g, Carbohydrates 53 g, Fiber 3 g, Fat 6 g, Saturated Fat 1 g, Cholesterol 166 mg, Sodium 559 mg (Analyzed with plain rice and Hot New Mexican Table Salsa.)

Quickie Dallas Dog

Using a tortilla instead of a bun and a spicy salsa instead of mustard, catsup, and pickle relish makes this a fun hot dog. Prepared in a microwave oven, these are easy as a wink and popular with almost anyone who likes hot dogs. You can add the same kinds of toppings as you would for tacos.

PREPARATION TIME: 1 minute in a microwave oven, 5 minutes conventionally
YIELD: 1 serving

1 (8-inch) flour tortilla
1 hot dog, any kind
2 Tablespoons spicy salsa

Optional Garnishes

Shredded cheese
Diced onion
Coleslaw

Place the tortilla on a paper towel and place the hot dog in the middle of the tortilla with the top at one end. Spoon the salsa over the top and sides of the hot dog. Fold the tortilla over the bottom of the hot dog. Wrap the side of the tortilla closest to you over the hot dog, then bring the far side tightly over the top. Roll the tortilla in the paper towel. Place in the microwave oven and cook for 1 minute on high power. Serve with cheese, onion, and coleslaw, if desired.

NOTE: To cook conventionally, boil the hot dog in water on top of the range for about 5 minutes or until done. Or slice the hot dog in half lengthwise (to speed up the cooking) and place it under the broiler on a piece of aluminum foil. Broil or grill them on high for 3 to 5 minutes per side. Place the hot dog in the tortilla with the salsa as described above. Serve with the cheese, onion, and coleslaw, if desired.

PER SERVING: Calories 336, Protein 11 g, Carbohydrates 28 g, Fiber 2 g, Fat 20 g, Saturated Fat 7 g, Cholesterol 34 mg, Sodium 889 mg

Crab Chard Wraps

Crab should be treated simply and with great respect. If you want to eat this dish out of hand, just wrap it in a warm corn tortilla.

PREPARATION TIME: 5 to 7 minutes
YIELD: 4 servings

    4 large leaves red-veined Swiss chard, well-rinsed
1/2 pound cooked crab or surimi (imitation crab)
    1 Tablespoon freshly squeezed lime juice (about 1/2 lime)
    4 scallions, including tender green parts, chopped
    2 cups cooked pasta, such as fusilli, or cooked rice*
       Jalapeño Lime Creme Dressing (recipe on page 48) for garnish, optional

Place the chard leaves in a plastic bag or a bowl, cover with waxed paper or plastic wrap, and cook in the microwave oven on high power for about 1 minute, or until the leaves wilt. Or drop the leaves into rapidly boiling water and cook conventionally for about 2 minutes.

Combine the crab, lime juice, scallions, and pasta in a bowl. Taste and add seasonings, if desired. Divide the crab mixture among the leaves; roll up and secure each with a toothpick.

To eat out of hand, enclose each wrap in a corn tortilla that has been warmed on a burner, or comal (cast iron griddle), or in a plastic bag in the microwave oven for 20 seconds. If desired, serve napped with the Jalapeño Lime Creme Dressing.

* See page xii about cooking pasta and rice in advance. It adds a great deal of convenience and speed to meals.

PER SERVING: Calories 171, Protein 16 g, Carbohydrates 23 g, Fiber 2 g, Fat 2 g, Saturated Fat 0 g, Cholesterol 57 mg, Sodium 263 mg

Swiss Chard–Wrapped Salmon

Chard leaves are so big that they make a great wrap.

COOKING TIME: 3 to 4 minutes in a microwave oven, 12 to 15 minutes in a conventional oven
YIELD: 4 servings

- 4 large leaves Swiss chard, well-rinsed
- 1 pound salmon fillet or steak, bones removed
- 4 teaspoons minced reconstituted chipotle chiles (see page 59) or 2 teaspoons chipotle powder
- 1 lime, cut into 8 slices

Place the chard leaves in a plastic bag and cook on high in the microwave oven for about 1 minute or until they wilt. Or immerse the leaves in rapidly boiling water for about 2 minutes. Drain the leaves and lay them flat on a work surface. Cut the salmon into 4 equal portions and place one on each leaf.

Place 1 teaspoon chipotles on each fillet and spread as uniformly as possible. Top each fillet with 2 slices of lime. Wrap the chard leaf around the fillets and secure with toothpicks, if needed.

Place the salmon wraps on a microwave-safe plate, cover with waxed paper or plastic wrap, and cook in the microwave oven on high power for 2 to 3 minutes, until done.* The thinner the cut of salmon, the faster it will cook. The salmon should be somewhat shiny in the center for the best flavor. Serve hot.

* To cook the salmon conventionally, preheat the oven to 425°F (220°C). Place the wraps on a baking sheet and cover with aluminum foil. Cook for 10 minutes.

PER SERVING: Calories 182, Protein 22 g, Carbohydrates 3 g, Fiber 1 g, Fat 9 g, Saturated Fat 2 g, Cholesterol 68 mg, Sodium 155 mg

Lettuce Lovers' Chimis

Iceberg lettuce has been shunned lately as being too plain. However, as a wrap and a texture for quickly prepared hot foods, it cannot be beat.

PREPARATION TIME: 6 to 8 minutes
YIELD: 4 servings

1/2	cup diced onion
1	pound ground turkey breast
1/4	cup Tomatillo Salsa (recipe on page 160)
8	outer leaves iceberg lettuce

In a heavy, nonstick or seasoned skillet, sauté the onion over medium-high heat without stirring for the first 2 minutes, until the onion is limp and somewhat caramelized. Reduce the heat to medium-low and add the turkey, breaking it up as you add it. Cook, stirring for 2 to 3 minutes, until the turkey just becomes white. Do not overcook. Remove the pan from the heat and add the salsa.

Place the lettuce leaves on 4 plates or on a work surface. Center the filling on each leaf. Serve, or warm in a microwave oven for about 30 seconds per serving or in a 400°F (200°C) oven for 2 to 3 minutes total.

PER SERVING: Calories 171, Protein 24 g, Carbohydrates 3 g, Fiber 1 g, Fat 6 g, Saturated Fat 2 g, Cholesterol 60 mg, Sodium 55 mg

Cumin Chicken Chimi

The heady scent of freshly ground cumin crosses many cultures but is particularly good in Southwestern dishes. A must in chili con carne, it is equally appropriate with this wonderful chicken filling. I have taken liberties calling this a chimi because it is not baked or fried. This is a "Sunday Best" recipe.

COOKING TIME: 4 to 6 minutes
YIELD: 4 servings

1	pound boneless, skinless chicken breasts or thighs
1	orange
3	cloves garlic
1 1/2	teaspoons freshly ground cumin
1/2	teaspoon crushed pequin quebrado or other hot red chile
8	corn tortillas
	Cilantro Orange Sauce (recipe follows), optional

Trim the chicken of any excess fat and connective tissue and cut the meat into 1-inch chunks. Using a zester, remove the orange zest and juice the orange. In a bowl combine the orange juice, about 1 teaspoon of the zest (reserve the rest of the zest for the Cilantro Orange Sauce), the garlic, cumin, and chile. Add the chicken and stir to mix well. Allow to sit in the marinade for at least 10 minutes; 30 minutes is even better. Drain.

In a heavy, well-seasoned skillet over medium-high heat, brown the drained chicken for 2 to 3 minutes. Turn and brown the other side. Meanwhile, warm the tortillas in a plastic bag in the microwave oven for 1 minute, or individually over a burner or on a comal (cast iron griddle) for a few seconds per side, or wrapped in aluminum foil in a 425°F (220°C) oven for about 5 minutes or until hot and pliable.

Divide the chicken among the tortillas, roll up the tortillas, and place seam side down on serving plates. Nap with the Cilantro Orange Sauce, if desired.

CILANTRO ORANGE SAUCE

	Remaining orange zest
1/2	cup plain yogurt
	About 1 Tablespoon coarsely chopped cilantro

Place the zest, yogurt, and cilantro in a small bowl and mix well.

PER SERVING: Calories 258, Protein 26 g, Carbohydrates 29 g, Fiber 3 g, Fat 4 g, Saturated Fat 1 g, Cholesterol 63 mg, Sodium 141 mg (Analyzed with chicken breast.)

Grilled Lamb Soft Tacos

Lamb takes well to this garlicky ginger marinade. This dish is inspired by fusion cooking and complemented by the unexpected sweet heat of jalapeño jelly. Serve it with a simple fruit salad such as orange slices with red onion and poppy seed dressing.

COOKING TIME: 4 to 6 minutes
YIELD: 4 servings

   1 pound trimmed boneless leg of lamb or sirloin steaks
   3 cloves garlic, minced
   1 (1/2-inch) piece fresh ginger, peeled and minced
1/2 cup mild jalapeño jelly or jam, warmed*
   4 (8- to 10-inch) flour tortillas
      Cilantro Salsa (recipe on page 165) for garnish, optional

Cut the lamb into 1/2-inch slices. Combine the garlic, ginger, and jelly in a small bowl. Spread the ginger mixture on each slice of lamb.

Meanwhile, preheat an outdoor grill, a stovetop grill, or a heavy, seasoned skillet to medium-high heat. To cook, separate the lamb slices and place them on the grill or in the skillet; sear for 2 to 3 minutes per side, until medium-rare. Meanwhile, warm the tortillas in a plastic bag for 1 minute or briefly over a burner or on a comal (cast iron griddle). Divide the filling among the tortillas, and wrap each tortilla around the filling. Serve with a bowl of the salsa, if desired.

* Warm the jelly in a microwave oven for 30 seconds, or in a boiling water bath, until it liquefies.

PER SERVING: Calories 501, Protein 30 g, Carbohydrates 69 g, Fiber 3 g, Fat 12 g, Saturated Fat 4 g, Cholesterol 73 mg, Sodium 415 mg (Analyzed with 10-inch tortillas.)

Breakfast Wrap

One of our favorite alumni—Charles Moore, from Phoenix, Arizona, who attended one of our classes—shared this quick and easy favorite. For a nourishing breakfast on the run, you could make this wrap to munch on as a "cruise chew." This is a "Sunday Best" recipe.

COOKING TIME: 2 to 3 minutes
YIELD: 1 serving

- 2 large eggs
- 2 Tablespoons bacon bits or bacon-flavored soy texturized protein bits
- 3 stuffed green olives, sliced
- 1 fresh or pickled jalapeño chile, minced
- 1/2 teaspoon ground pure mild red chile powder
-    Nonstick oil spray
- 1 (8-inch) flour tortilla

Crack the eggs into a small bowl and whip. Add the bacon bits, olives, jalapeño, and chile powder and whisk again.

Lightly spray a heavy, well-seasoned skillet with nonstick oil spray and place over medium-low heat. Add the egg mixture and cook, stirring, until it is as firm as you like. Heat the tortilla briefly over the burner you were cooking on. Place the egg mixture in the center of the tortilla and roll it up. Serve immediately.

PER SERVING: Calories 379, Protein 23 g, Carbohydrates 30 g, Fiber 2 g, Fat 18 g, Saturated Fat 5 g, Cholesterol 434 mg, Sodium 1043 mg (Note: Bacon bits contribute 40 percent of the sodium and olives 23 percent.)

PER SERVING: Calories 330, Protein 27 g, Carbohydrates 30 g, Fiber 2 g, Fat 12 g, Saturated Fat 3 g, Cholesterol 11 mg, Sodium 1142 mg (Analyzed without the bacon bits and with liquid egg substitute.)

Fajita Favorites

Fajitas are at their best when simply made by marinating the meat in freshly squeezed lime juice, lots of freshly minced garlic, a little oil, and ground black pepper.

Another secret is to never slice the meat until after it is cooked. Fajitas prepared this way will be juicy and flavorful instead of dried out and dull.

For convenience I like to make lots of fajita filling at once and freeze it in one-serving portions. Although the original fajita was made with skirt steak, I like to make all kinds—including beef (see lamb recipe on page 30), chicken, turkey, duck, shrimp, and scallops.

Fajitas can be served several different ways. The meat fillings are also delicious on pizzas and in main-dish salads and quesadillas.

COOKING TIME: 4 to 8 minutes
YIELD: 4 servings

1 1/2 pounds lean, trimmed skirt steak; boneless, skinless chicken breast; or peeled, deveined, uncooked shrimp
1/4 cup freshly squeezed lime juice (1 large or 2 small limes)
4 cloves garlic, minced
2 Tablespoons vegetable oil or extra-virgin olive oil, preferably Spanish
Several grinds of black pepper, optional
4 (6- to 8-inch) flour tortillas, warmed (see page 2)

Optional Garnishes

Red onion
Red, yellow, and green bell pepper slices
Pico de Gallo (recipe on page 168)
Sour cream

Trim the beef or chicken. Pound the beef with a tenderizer mallet. Flatten the chicken with a French tenderizer-pounder or the side of a chef's knife or cleaver.

In a shallow bowl mix the lime juice, garlic, oil, and black pepper, if using. Allow to marinate about 10 minutes. If not cooking immediately, freeze in individual plastic bags.

Meanwhile, preheat the grill. Pan-sear the vegetables, or if grilling the vegetables, start with the onion, then the green peppers, and then grill the meat or shrimp. Cook the beef for about 3 minutes per side, or until rare. Cook the chicken for about 4 minutes per side. Cook the shrimp for about 2 minutes per side, or until the shrimp turn pink. Slice the beef or chicken across the grain into 1/2-inch-wide strips.

Place the beef, chicken, or shrimp in each warm tortilla. Top with the grilled green peppers and onions, if using, and roll up the tortillas. Serve with the pico de gallo and sour cream, if desired.

PER SERVING (beef fajitas): Calories 446, Protein 40 g, Carbohydrates 28 g, Fiber 2 g, Fat 18 g, Saturated Fat 7 g, Cholesterol 88 mg, Sodium 341 mg (Note: The fat can be trimmed with leaner meat, such as sirloin tip or chicken.)

PER SERVING (chicken fajitas): Calories 358, Protein 39 g, Carbohydrates 28 g, Fiber 2 g, Fat 9 g, Saturated Fat 2 g, Cholesterol 94 mg, Sodium 314 mg

PER SERVING (shrimp fajitas): Calories 298, Protein 30 g, Carbohydrates 28 g, Fiber 2 g, Fat 6 g, Saturated Fat 1 g, Cholesterol 242 mg, Sodium 511 mg

Caramelized Onion Wrap

Onions take on a new personality when they are slow-cooked in a heavy pan long enough to brown in their own juices. Add New Mexico's green chiles and other flavorings and wrap all in a steaming corn tortilla for a marvelous veggie snack or light meal. This is a "Sunday Best" recipe.

COOKING TIME: 8 to 10 minutes
YIELD: 4 servings

- 4 large onions, halved and thinly sliced
- 2 (4-ounce) cans chopped green chiles
- 3 cloves garlic, minced
- 3 Tablespoons nonfat sour cream
- 1/4 cup crumbled feta cheese or Mexican queso blanco
- 8 corn tortillas, warmed (see page 2)
  Cilantro sprigs for garnish, optional

In a heavy, seasoned skillet over medium-high heat, cook the onions, without stirring for a minute or 2, until the edges are slightly browned. Then stir and continue to cook until the onion caramelizes. Add the green chiles and garlic and cook for about 3 minutes, or until heated through.

Stir in the sour cream and cheese, then divide the filling among the warm tortillas, placing a strip of filling down the center of each. Roll up, garnish with cilantro, if desired, and serve.

PER SERVING: Calories 217, Protein 7 g, Carbohydrates 42 g, Fiber 6 g, Fat 4 g, Saturated Fat 2 g, Cholesterol 9 mg, Sodium 867 mg (Analyzed with feta cheese.)

*A "Sunday Best" recipe with more than five ingredients but fewer than ten.

VEGETARIAN DISHES

Southwestern ingredients lend themselves to flavorful vegetarian dishes. The spice of the chiles coupled with the nutritious fiber of the beans, corn, and other popular vegetables in the cuisine allow for an innovative range of delicious vegetarian dishes. I enjoy the challenge of taking the meat out even though I am a meat eater.

In addition to the vegetarian entrées I have included here, there are several vegetarian recipes among the other chapters. Check the index for their listings. And you can create many more vegetarian dishes for quick and easy Southwestern cooking by adapting the recipes in the other chapters.

Pasta Portobello Toss

Portobello mushrooms are so rich and flavorful that they can be a meal by themselves. If they are not available, shiitake or oyster mushrooms can be substituted. Or button mushrooms could be used. Fresh mushrooms have the best flavor; however, dried mushrooms can be used for part of the amount and will impart a greater depth of taste.

COOKING TIME: 8 to 10 minutes
YIELD: 3 or 4 servings

- 2 Tablespoons extra-virgin olive oil, preferably Spanish, divided
  About 2 cups sliced Portobello mushrooms (1 or 2 mushrooms)
  Freshly ground black pepper to taste
- 8 ounces dry, uncooked spaghetti-type pasta
- 6 cloves garlic, minced
- 1 medium zucchini, unpeeled, sliced into 1/2-inch rounds

Bring a large pot of salted water to a boil for pasta. Meanwhile, in a medium skillet with deep sides, heat 1 Tablespoon of the oil. Cook the mushrooms, adding the ground pepper and garlic. Remove the mushrooms to a bowl when soft (about 3 to 4 minutes); reserve the pan.

Cook the pasta according to package directions, adding the zucchini after 3 minutes of cooking. Drain the pasta and zucchini and add them, along with the reserved mushrooms, to the pan in which the mushrooms were cooked. Toss with remaining oil and serve.

PER SERVING (1/4 recipe): Calories 301, Protein 9 g, Carbohydrates 49 g, Fiber 5 g, Fat 8 g, Saturated Fat 1 g, Cholesterol 0 mg, Sodium 4 mg

Hot Pasta with Broccoli

This basic recipe can be used as a guide for other vegetables such as zucchini, eggplant, or asparagus—even cooked dried beans such as pintos or black beans. If you do not have cooked pasta, boil the water for it first and cook the broccoli in the boiling water. This is a "Sunday Best" recipe.

COOKING TIME: 5 minutes
YIELD: 4 servings

5 ounces dry, uncooked red, green, or white chile fusilli pasta (4 cups cooked)
2 cups broccoli florets (2 large heads)
1 Tablespoon extra-virgin olive oil, preferably Spanish
1 large onion, cut into 1/2-inch dice
2 large cloves garlic, minced
2 teaspoons crushed red caribe chiles
Grated Romano cheese for garnish, optional

Bring a large pot of salted water to a boil and cook the pasta according to package directions, adding the broccoli for the last five minutes. Drain and set aside.

In a large skillet heat the oil. Add the onion and sauté for 2 to 3 minutes, until the onion is golden. Add the garlic and cook for about 3 minutes. Add the cooked pasta and chiles and, reducing heat to medium-low, continue heating, tossing to warm evenly. Serve with the cheese, if desired.

PER SERVING: Calories 172, Protein 6 g, Carbohydrates 29 g, Fiber 3 g, Fat 4 g, Saturated Fat 1 g, Cholesterol 0 mg, Sodium 13 mg

Southwestern Vegetable Lasagna

Substituting corn tortillas for the lasagna noodles and layering with vegetables makes for a quick and tasty main dish. There is lots of room for substitution. If you don't like or don't have on hand refried pinto beans, for example, you can use another starchy vegetable, such as corn, garbanzos, or other beans. Zucchini can also be substituted.

COOKING TIME: 15 to 20 minutes
YIELD: 4 servings

      Nonstick oil spray
1 1/2 cups tomato-based salsa, divided
   8 corn tortillas, divided
   1 (15-ounce) can refried pinto beans
   1 (10-ounce) package frozen spinach, thawed
   1 cup nonfat sour cream, divided

Preheat the oven to 375°F (190°C). Lightly spray an 8 x 8-inch baking dish with nonstick oil spray. Spread a couple of spoonsful of salsa in the dish and top with 4 of the tortillas, arranging them in a uniform layer. In a bowl combine the beans, spinach, and 3/4 cup of the sour cream. Spread half of the mixture evenly over the tortillas. Top with half of the remaining salsa.

Arrange the remaining tortillas evenly over the bean mixture and cover with the rest of the bean mixture. Top with the balance of the salsa. Place a dollop of the reserved sour cream over the salsa. Bake for 15 to 20 minutes, until the top of the "lasagna" bubbles. Serve hot.

PER SERVING: Calories 334, Protein 16 g, Carbohydrates 63 g, Fiber 12 g, Fat 3 g, Saturated Fat 1 g, Cholesterol 14 mg, Sodium 608 mg

Quickie Tamale Pie

Tamale pies have long been a favorite buffet and entertainment dish. Using the convenience of pre-cooked cornmeal, often labeled polenta, cuts the preparation time.

COOKING TIME: 20 minutes
YIELD: 4 servings

     Nonstick oil spray
1 (12-ounce) package or can prepared cornmeal mush (polenta)
1 (15-ounce) can pinto or black beans, drained
1 (15-ounce) can whole kernel corn, drained
1 cup tomato-based salsa
1/2 cup mixed shredded Monterey Jack and Cheddar cheeses

Preheat the oven to 425°F (220°C). Lightly spray an 8 x 8-inch baking dish with nonstick oil spray. Evenly spread the cornmeal into the dish. In a bowl combine the beans, corn, and salsa; spoon over the cornmeal. Sprinkle with the cheeses and bake for about 20 minutes, or until bubbly. Serve hot.

PER SERVING: Calories 387, Protein 19 g, Carbohydrates 60 g, Fiber 11 g, Fat 10 g, Saturated Fat 5 g, Cholesterol 29 mg, Sodium 716 mg (Analyzed with pinto beans.)

Pasta Toss with Seared Veggies and Black Beans

The trick to pan-searing vegetables is to heat a heavy skillet to medium-high heat and add the most liquid vegetable first. This is a "Sunday Best" recipe.

COOKING TIME: 12 to 15 minutes
YIELD: 4 servings

- 10 ounces dry, uncooked red chile rotini pasta or plain rotini pasta and 2 Tablespoons ground pure hot red chile (4 cups cooked pasta)
- 1 large red onion, sliced vertically into thin wedges
- 1 zucchini, sliced into 1/4-inch-thick rounds
- 1 red bell pepper, cut into thin strips
- 3 cloves garlic, minced
- 1 (15-ounce) can black beans, drained

If cooked pasta is not available, bring a large pot of salted water to a boil and cook the pasta according to package directions. Drain and set aside.

In the meantime, in a heavy, well-seasoned skillet over medium-high heat, cook the onion, without stirring for a minute or 2, until the edges start to brown. Stir and add the zucchini, red peppers, and garlic. Cook, stirring, until the vegetables are done.

Add the beans and heat together. Add the cooked pasta and toss together in the skillet to mix and warm evenly. Taste and adjust the seasonings. Serve hot.

VARIATION: For more flavor, add 1 to 2 Tablespoons balsamic vinegar or red wine vinegar.

PER SERVING: Calories 382, Protein 17 g, Carbohydrates 75 g, Fiber 12 g, Fat 2 g, Saturated Fat 0 g, Cholesterol 0 mg, Sodium 213 mg

Blackened Fresh Tomato Southwestern Pasta

Fresh tomatoes right from the garden are always best. My favorite are Romas. The secret to the special sweet, rich flavor of this sauce is caramelizing the onions and charring the tomatoes. Oil-cured or Greek olives, beans of any kind, cubed eggplant, zucchini, or any other seasonal vegetable you have on hand can be added. This is a "Sunday Best" recipe.

COOKING TIME: 10 to 15 minutes
YIELD: 4 servings

  4 Roma tomatoes, roasted under a broiler until blackened*
  1 onion, diced
  3 cloves garlic, minced
  2 dried chipotle chiles, reconstituted (see page 59) and minced, or 1 teaspoon ground chipotle
 1/2 teaspoon dried, ground, or crushed Mexican oregano
10 to 12 ounces dry, green chile or plain pasta of any type

Bring a large pot of salted water to a boil for cooking the pasta. Peel and dice the blackened tomatoes.

Cook the pasta according to package directions. In a heavy, seasoned skillet over medium-high heat, cook the onion, not stirring for a minute or 2, until the edges brown a bit, then stir and add the tomatoes. Add the garlic, chiles, and oregano. Reduce the heat to low and simmer for about 5 minutes.

Drain and add to the tomato mixture. Stir together and serve.

* If preferred, you can blacken the tomatoes over a burner on top of the range. Frozen blackened tomatoes can also be used.

PER SERVING: Calories 147, Protein 5 g, Carbohydrates 30 g, Fiber 3 g, Fat 1 g, Saturated Fat 0 g, Cholesterol 0 mg, Sodium 16 mg (Analyzed with 2 1/2 ounces of pasta.)

Pueblo Indian Corn and Pumpkin Stew

Corn and pumpkin were popular mainstays of the Native American diet. Here they are married for a flavorful stew. Time permitting, fresh grilled corn cut off the cob is best. Serve the stew with warm corn tortillas. This is a "Sunday Best" recipe.

COOKING TIME: 10 minutes
YIELD: 4 servings

1 (14 1/2-ounce) can vegetable stock
1 (15-ounce) can whole kernel corn, drained (approximately 1 1/2 cups)
1 (15-ounce) can pumpkin
1 (8-ounce) can tomato sauce
2 Tablespoons ground pure hot red New Mexican chile or to taste
1 teaspoon ground cumin
   Nonfat sour cream for garnish, optional
   Crushed red caribe chile for garnish, optional

In a 3-quart saucepan, combine the stock, corn, pumpkin, tomato sauce, ground chile, and cumin. Simmer for about 10 minutes. Taste and adjust the seasonings. Serve garnished with a dollop of sour cream sprinkled with caribe chile, if desired.

PER SERVING: Calories 137, Protein 5 g, Carbohydrates 31 g, Fiber 7 g, Fat 2 g, Saturated Fat 0 g, Cholesterol 0 mg, Sodium 703 mg (Analyzed without optional ingredients.)

Black Bean and Red Chile Flat Enchiladas

Once, for a vegan vegetarian friend in New York City, I served these enchiladas with crisp-fried tofu squares instead of cheese and they were absolutely delicious. These flat, New Mexico–style enchiladas can be garnished with lettuce and chopped tomato to make a light meal.

BAKING TIME: 12 to 15 minutes
YIELD: 4 servings

- 2 cups Basic Red Chile Sauce (recipe on page 156) made with vegetable stock
- 8 corn tortillas, preferably blue
- 1/2 cup medium-fine diced onion
- 1 (15-ounce) can black beans, drained
- 1 cup shredded Cheddar cheese or 8 ounces tofu cut into 1/2-inch squares and crisp-fried in 1 to 2 Tablespoons cooking oil
  Coarsely chopped romaine lettuce for garnish, optional
  Chopped tomato for garnish, optional

Preheat the oven to 425°F (220°C). Place a spoonful of sauce on 4 ovenproof plates. Top with a tortilla, then a spoonful of sauce, a layer of onion, one-eighth of the black beans, and one-eighth of the cheese or tofu. Repeat, placing a tortilla on top of the final layer of cheese. Bake for 12 to 15 minutes, until bubbly. Serve immediately encircled with the lettuce and chopped tomato, if desired.

PER SERVING: Calories 429, Protein 20 g, Carbohydrates 56 g, Fiber 14 g, Fat 15 g, Saturated Fat 8 g, Cholesterol 37 g, Sodium 643 mg
PER SERVING: Calories 364, Protein 20 g, Carbohydrates 56 g, Fiber 14 g, Fat 8 g, Saturated Fat 3 g, Cholesterol 14 mg, Sodium 474 mg (Analyzed with a low-fat cheese.)

Pinto Pies with Salsa

The earthy, rich flavor of pinto beans when sautéed with "tinged" or lightly tanned garlic is wonderful. It can be served as a light meal most any time of day. This is a "Sunday Best" recipe.

COOKING TIME: 12 to 15 minutes
YIELD: 4 servings

    3   teaspoons extra-virgin olive oil, preferably Spanish
    4   cloves garlic, minced
  1/4   cup finely diced onion
    2   (15-ounce) cans vegetarian, low-fat, refried pinto beans
    1   dried chipotle chile, reconstituted (see page 59) and diced, or 1 teaspoon chipotle powder, or 1 teaspoon minced fresh jalapeño chile
  1/4   cup cornmeal, any kind
    1   cup tomato-based salsa

In a heavy, seasoned skillet, warm 1 teaspoon of the oil. Sauté the garlic and onion until they are lightly browned. Add the beans and chipotle and cook, stirring, until the mixture is very thick. Remove from the skillet and set aside. Reserve the skillet.

Cover a baking sheet with wax paper or aluminum foil. Lightly sprinkle with the cornmeal. Dust your hands with cornmeal, then shape the bean mixture into 8 pies, each about 1/2 inch thick. Place each on the baking sheet and dust with more cornmeal.

Pour the remaining 2 teaspoons of oil into the skillet and heat to medium-high. Add the pies and cook for 6 to 8 minutes, until crispy, then turn and cook for 3 to 4 minutes, until browned. Serve two per person on a bed of salsa.

PER SERVING: Calories 271, Protein 13 g, Carbohydrates 42 g, Fiber 13 g, Fat 6 g, Saturated Fat 1 g, Cholesterol 0 mg, Sodium 953 mg (Note: 85 percent of the sodium is from the canned refried beans. Home-cooked beans can be much lower in sodium.)

Black Bean Green Chili

Black beans are a relative newcomer to the Southwestern heartland. Originating in the Caribbean, they are a perfect accompaniment to New Mexico's green chiles. This is a "Sunday Best" recipe.

COOKING TIME: 10 minutes
YIELD: 4 servings

   2 (4-ounce) cans chopped green chiles, undrained*
   1 (15-ounce) can black beans
   1 red bell pepper, cut into 1/2-inch dice
   1 (14 1/2-ounce) can low-sodium vegetable broth
   2 cloves garlic, minced
1 1/2 teaspoons freshly ground cumin
   1 lime

In a 3-quart saucepan, combine the undrained chiles, black beans, red pepper, broth, garlic, and cumin. Simmer for 10 minutes. To serve, place in 4 soup bowls and squeeze lime over each serving.

* If you'd like a hotter chili, add ground pure hot red chile to taste.

NOTE: For a deeper, richer taste, caramelize a diced onion and add to the chili.

PER SERVING: Calories 132, Protein 9 g, Carbohydrates 23 g, Fiber 6 g, Fat 2 g, Saturated Fat 0 g, Cholesterol 2 mg, Sodium 425 mg

Baked Veggie Chimichangas

Chimichangas—the word, literally translated, means "bites for my loved one"—have been a favorite Southwestern dish for several years. Originally deep-fried and smothered with sour cream, guacamole, and salsas, they taste equally good when baked and simply sauced with salsa. This is a "Sunday Best" recipe.

COOKING TIME: 12 to 15 minutes
YIELD: 4 servings

1	(15-ounce) can pinto or black beans, well-drained
1	(4-ounce) can diced green chiles, drained
1/2	cup shredded cabbage or coleslaw mix
1/2	cup nonfat sour cream, divided
1	cup tomato- or tomatillo-based salsa, divided
4	(10-inch) flour tortillas, warmed (see page 2)

Preheat the oven to 425°F (220°C). In a medium glass bowl combine the beans, chiles, cabbage, 1/4 cup of the sour cream, and 1/4 cup of the salsa. Cover and process on high power in the microwave for 2 minutes or simmer 3 to 5 minutes in a heavy pan on top of the range.

Lay each of the warm tortillas on a baking sheet. Spoon the filling down the center of each, about 1 1/2 inches in from the bottom of the tortilla and 1 inch in from each side. Bring the bottom up over the filling, tuck in each side, and roll up. Secure with toothpicks. Place seam side down on the baking sheet.

Bake for 12 to 15 minutes, until lightly browned. Remove the toothpicks and serve belted with the remaining 3/4 cup salsa. Place a small dollop of the remaining sour cream in the center of each.

PER SERVING: Calories 419, Protein 17 g, Carbohydrates 75 g, Fiber 11 g, Fat 6 g, Saturated Fat 1 g, Cholesterol 3 mg, Sodium mg

Spinach and Corn Rolled Enchiladas

Seared corn or leftover grilled corn definitely sets this sauce apart. This is a "Sunday Best" recipe.

COOKING TIME: 20 minutes
YIELD: 4 servings

- 2 ears Mexican-Style Grilled Corn (recipe on page 120) or 1 (10-ounce) package frozen corn kernels
- 1 cup evaporated skim milk
- 3 cloves garlic, minced
  Nonstick oil spray
- 8 corn tortillas, warmed (see page 2)
- 1 (15-ounce) can spinach, without salt, well-drained
- 1/2 cup chopped onion
- 1 cup shredded low-fat Monterey Jack cheese

Cut the grilled corn from the cob. If using frozen corn, place it in a heavy, seasoned skillet over medium-high heat to brown. In a blender combine the milk, garlic, and corn. Process until smooth. Transfer to a shallow plate.

Preheat the oven to 400°F (200°C). Lightly spray an 8 x 8-inch baking dish with nonstick oil spray. Dip each warm tortilla in the corn mixture. Place on a flat surface and sprinkle with one-eighth of the spinach, onion, and cheese, reserving some cheese for garnish. Roll, then place seam side down in the baking dish. Cover with the rest of the corn mixture, making sure that you pour it evenly over each enchilada. Sprinkle with the reserved cheese. Bake for 10 minutes or until bubbly. Serve hot.

PER SERVING: Calories 330, Protein 21 g, Carbohydrates 47 g, Fiber 7 g, Fat 9 g, Saturated Fat 4 g, Cholesterol 23 mg, Sodium 413 mg

*A "Sunday Best" recipe with more than five ingredients but fewer than ten.

SAUCES, SALSAS GALORE, AND SPICY PANTRY PLEASURES

Sauces, especially salsas, are the essence of Southwestern cookery. They are flavorful, always spicy, low in fat, and a wonderful flavor and appearance enhancer for most any entrée. Lots of the flavor and personality in Southwestern foods comes from the salsas, sauces, and zesty glazes that make the dish.

Included in this chapter are several easy recipes for making salsas and sauces to help you transform your own creations into Southwestern favorites. I've also added a few other special recipes for my favorite Basic Rub (recipe on page 173), Hot Honey (recipe on page 174), and a fabulous Zippy Glaze (recipe on page 172).

Basic Red Chile Sauce

This is my favorite red chile sauce, which is the basis for enchiladas and for saucing over chiles rellenos, tamales, and traditional Southwestern specialties. You'll notice that I make my red sauce from chile powder. High-quality, ground pure chile powders are so much faster, consistent, and nutritious than cooking with pods, whose exact flavor potential is impossible to know due to the random nature of chiles. This is a "Sunday Best" recipe.

PREPARATION TIME: about 15 minutes
YIELD: 2 cups, or 4 servings

1	Tablespoon unsalted butter or lard
2	Tablespoons all-purpose flour
1/4	cup ground pure mild red New Mexican chile powder
2 to 4	Tablespoons ground pure hot red New Mexican chile powder
2	cups stock (beef, chicken, or vegetable)
1	clove garlic, minced
	Pinch each of ground or dried Mexican oregano
	Pinch of freshly ground cumin
	Salt, optional

In a heavy saucepan melt the butter. Add the flour and cook, stirring, until the mixture turns slightly golden. Remove the pan from the cooking heat and stir in the chile powders. Stir in the stock. Continue stirring until the mixture becomes smooth. Add the garlic, oregano, and cumin and simmer for about 10 minutes. Taste and adjust the seasonings, adding salt, if desired.

VARIATION: Ground chuck, roast beef, pork, cheese, or poached chicken or turkey can be added when making enchiladas.

PER SERVING: Calories 90, Protein 3 g, Carbohydrates 12 g, Fiber 4 g, Fat 4 g, Saturated Fat 2 g, Cholesterol 8 mg, Sodium 363 mg (Analyzed with butter.) (Note: To reduce sodium, use low-sodium stock or water.)

Favorite Green Chile Sauce

Some people like to make green chile sauce with tomatoes. I have always thought that the taste of the chiles came through a lot better with a chicken or vegetable stock base. You can use this sauce as is to make enchiladas or to sauce burritos and the like. Or you can add poached chicken or seafood to the sauce. This is a "Sunday Best" recipe.

COOKING TIME: about 15 minutes
YIELD: about 2 cups, or 4 servings

- 1 Tablespoon unsalted butter or lard
- 1/2 cup chopped onion
- 2 Tablespoons all-purpose flour
- 1 1/2 cups chicken or vegetable stock
- 1 cup parched (instructions page xvii) and chopped green chiles, or 2 (4-ounce) cans green chiles, drained
- 1 large clove garlic, finely minced
  Salt, optional

In a heavy saucepan, melt the butter. Add the onion and sauté until it is clear. Add the flour, gradually stir in the stock, and cook until the mixture is smooth. Add the chiles and garlic and simmer for 10 minutes. Taste and adjust the seasonings, adding salt, if desired.

PER SERVING: Calories 71, Protein 3 g, Carbohydrates 8 g, Fiber 1 g, Fat 4 g, Saturated Fat 2 g, Cholesterol 10 mg, Sodium 74 mg

Hot New Mexican Table Salsa

Sometimes known as salsa roja or salsa colorado, this salsa is the most popular in traditional New Mexican restaurants because it has a great flavor and keeps well.

PREPARATION TIME: 5 minutes
YIELD: 1 3/4 cup, or 3 to 6 servings

- 1 (14 1/2-ounce) can peeled whole tomatoes (with no added herbs or seasonings), diced, or diced canned tomatoes
- 2 teaspoons finely crushed red pequin chile or to taste
- 2 Tablespoons cider vinegar
- 1 1/2 teaspoons ground cumin
- 2 cloves garlic, minced

In a bowl combine the tomatoes, chile, vinegar, cumin, and garlic. Allow to stand for at least 10 minutes before serving.

VARIATIONS: Substitute 1 Tablespoon freshly squeezed lime juice for 1 Tablespoon of the cider vinegar. Add a generous pinch of chopped fresh Mexican oregano and some coarsely chopped cilantro, if desired.

PER SERVING (1/6 recipe): Calories 28, Protein 1 g, Carbohydrates 6 g, Fiber 2 g, Fat 0 g, Saturated Fat 0 g, Cholesterol 0 mg, Sodium 92 mg

Salsa Fresca

The original salsa—commemorating the Mexican flag—was made with equal parts of red, green, and white: red tomatoes, green chiles, and white onions. This versatile salsa is about as good as it gets for most everything—as a dipping salsa, over meats of any kind, as a base for salsa vinaigrette (salad dressing), or on traditional dishes such as tacos and burritos. Should any ever be left, make it into a salad dressing or freeze it for use in chile con queso or as a sauce for huevos rancheros.

PREPARATION TIME: 10 minutes
YIELD: 3 cups, or 4 to 6 servings

- 1 cup red, ripe tomato chopped into 1/2-inch dice
- 1 cup white Spanish onion chopped into 1/4-inch dice
- 1 cup parched (instructions on page xvii), peeled, and chopped green chiles or 2 (4-ounce) cans green chiles, drained
- 1 clove garlic, minced
- 1/2 cup coarsely chopped cilantro
  Salt, optional

In a bowl combine the tomato, onion, chiles, garlic, and cilantro. Allow to stand for about 10 minutes before serving. Taste and add salt, if desired.

PER SERVING (1/6 recipe): Calories 27, Protein 1 g, Carbohydrates 6 g, Fiber 1 g, Fat 0 g, Saturated Fat 0 g, Cholesterol 0 mg, Sodium 6 mg

Tomatillo Salsa (Mexican Salsa Verde)

Tomatillos, which are distantly related to tomatoes, have a fruity, fresh flavor that complements most any food or dish they accompany.

PREPARATION TIME: 15 minutes
YIELD: about 1 1/2 cups, or 4 servings

> About 8 ounces fresh tomatillos (1 1/2 cups husked)
> 1 fresh jalapeño chile
> 1 (2-inch) wedge fresh onion (about 1/4 cup onion)
> 1/4 cup fresh cilantro leaves (including tops of stalks)
> Salt, optional

Pour about an inch of water into a saucepan with a lid and bring to a boil. Meanwhile, husk the tomatillos, rinse, and cut the larger ones to be the same size as the others for even cooking. Cook the tomatillos for 5 to 7 minutes, until fork-tender. Drain, reserving some of the liquid. Place the tomatillos, jalapeño, onion, and cilantro in a blender or food processor and process until pureed. Taste and adjust the seasonings, adding salt and more jalapeño or cilantro, if desired.

PER SERVING: Calories 23, Protein 1 g, Carbohydrates 4 mg, Fiber 1 g, Fat 1 g, Saturated Fat 0 g, Cholesterol 0 mg, Sodium 2 mg

Cucumber Salsa

This salsa is excellent with most any seafood. I particularly like it belted over salmon.

PREPARATION TIME: about 5 minutes
YIELD: about 2 cups, or 4 servings

1 medium cucumber, scored with a fork and thinly sliced*
1 medium sweet white onion, finely diced
1 Tablespoon freshly squeezed lime juice (about 1/2 lime)
1 teaspoon crushed red caribe chile

In a medium bowl combine the cucumber, onion, lime juice, and chile, and toss together. Allow to marinate for a few minutes before serving.

* To score a cucumber with a fork, hold the tines firmly against the skin and pull the fork along the length of the cucumber. Repeat until the entire outside of the cucumber is scored.

PER SERVING: Calories 24, Protein 1 g, Carbohydrates 5 g, Fiber 1 g, Fat 0 g, Saturated Fat 0 g, Cholesterol 0 mg, Sodium 2 mg

Chipotle Cantaloupe Salsa

This salsa could be used as a dipping salsa with vegetables or chips. The smoky chipotle stands up to the perfumey cantaloupe. I am particularly fond of this salsa over the Blue Corn–Crusted Red Snapper (recipe on page 85).

PREPARATION TIME: 5 to 7 minutes
YIELD: about 2 cups, or 4 servings

 1 dried chipotle chile, reconstituted (see page 59) and finely chopped, or 1/2 teaspoon powdered chipotle
 1 medium red onion, diced
1/2 cantaloupe, peeled and cut into 1/2-inch cubes
 1 Tablespoon freshly squeezed lime juice (about 1/2 lime)
 2 Tablespoons coarsely chopped cilantro

In a medium bowl combine the chipotle, onion, cantaloupe, lime juice, and cilantro; stir together. Taste, and if desired, add some of the stewing liquid from the chipotles or if using powder add more fresh lime juice if desired.

PER SERVING: Calories 36, Protein 1 g, Carbohydrates 9 g, Fiber 1 g, Fat 0 g, Saturated Fat 0 g, Cholesterol 0 mg, Sodium 7 mg

Mango Salsa

The gingery peach flavor of ripe, pungent mangos is wonderful with any mild-flavored seafood or poultry. You could also serve this as a dipping salsa with jicama or corn chips.

PREPARATION TIME: 5 to 7 minutes
YIELD: 1 1/2 cups, or 3 or 4 servings

3/4	cup mango chopped into 1/2-inch cubes
3/4	cup diced Spanish onion
1/4	cup coarsely chopped cilantro
2	Tablespoons balsamic vinegar
1	teaspoon or more crushed red pequin quebrado

Place the mango, onion, cilantro, vinegar, and chile in a bowl and toss together. Taste and determine if you wish to add more pequin. Allow the flavors to blend for at least 10 to 15 minutes before serving.

PER SERVING: Calories 41, Protein 1 g, Carbohydrates 10 g, Fiber 2 g, Fat 0 g, Saturated Fat 0 g, Cholesterol 0 mg, Sodium 6 mg

Sweet Pear Piña Salsa

The mellow flavor of pears makes them an excellent backdrop for the sweet pineapple contrasted with the somewhat tart dried cranberries and the piquant pequin. This salsa is excellent with pork, poultry, or seafood.

PREPARATION TIME: 5 to 7 minutes
YIELD: about 2 1/2 cups, or 4 generous servings

1	D'Anjou or Bartlett pear, peeled, cored, and diced
1	(8-ounce) can crushed pineapple, drained
1	cup dried cranberries or Craisins
1/2	teaspoon crushed red pequin quebrado or more to taste

In a nonreactive bowl combine the pear, pineapple, cranberries, and chile. Allow to stand for at least 10 minutes before serving.

PER SERVING: Calories 78, Protein 0 g, Carbohydrates 0 g, Fiber 2 g, Fat 0 g, Saturated Fat 0 g, Cholesterol 0 mg, Sodium 145 mg

Cilantro Salsa

This fresh-tasting salsa is terrific over chilled salmon, as well as with most any other seafood or poultry dish.

PREPARATION TIME: 5 minutes
YIELD: about 1 3/4 cup, or 4 servings

1/2	cup chopped onion
1	cup chopped red bell pepper
1	small jalapeño chile, minced
1/4	cup coarsely chopped cilantro
2	Tablespoons lemon juice

In a nonreactive bowl combine the onion, red pepper, jalapeño, cilantro, and lemon juice. Allow to stand for at least 10 minutes before serving.

PER SERVING: Calories 22, Protein 1 g, Carbohydrates 5 g, Fiber 1 g, Fat 0 g, Saturated Fat 0 g, Cholesterol 0 mg, Sodium 2 mg

Cilantro Pesto

The fresh taste of cilantro complements the spiciness of chile. You'll find that this pesto is terrific in dishes such as the Chevre Wrap (recipe on page 127) and on most any pasta. You can even add more olive oil and vinegar in equal parts for a delicious salad dressing. This is a "Sunday Best" recipe.

PREPARATION TIME: 3 to 5 minutes
YIELD: 1 cup

- 1/4 cup extra-virgin olive oil, preferably Spanish
- 1 cup loosely packed cilantro leaves
- 2 Tablespoons roasted piñons
- 2 large cloves garlic
- 1 fresh jalapeño chile
- 1/3 cup grated Romano or Parmesan cheese

In a blender combine the oil, cilantro, piñons, garlic, jalapeño, and cheese. Process until smooth. This pesto will keep 3 to 4 weeks in the refrigerator or 6 months in the freezer.

PER SERVING (1/4 cup): Calories 184, Protein 3 g, Carbohydrates 2 g, Fiber 1 g, Fat 18 g, Saturated Fat 4 g, Cholesterol 9 mg, Sodium 105 mg (Analyzed with Romano cheese.)

Plum Pico de Gallo

The traditional salsa for fajitas, originally made with tomatoes, can be adapted to other fruits, such as plums, peaches, nectarines, strawberries, or melon.

PREPARATION TIME: 10 minutes
YIELD: about 1 1/2 cups, or 3 or 4 servings

   2 dried chipotle chiles, reconstituted (see page 59), plus 2 Tablespoons of the juice, or 1 teaspoon chipotle powder and 2 Tablespoons freshly squeezed lime juice (1 lime)
   1 cup diced fresh plums (3 to 4 plums)
1/2 cup chopped onion (1/2 onion)
   2 cloves garlic, minced
   2 Tablespoons coarsely chopped cilantro
      Lime juice, optional when using the chipotle pods

In a bowl combine the chiles and juice, the plums, onion, garlic, and cilantro. When using the chipotle pods, add a squeeze of lime juice, if desired. Set aside for 5 to 10 minutes for the flavors to blend.

PER SERVING (1/4 recipe): Calories 34, Protein 1 g, Carbohydrates 8 g, Fiber 1 g, Fat 0 g, Saturated Fat 0 g, Cholesterol 0 mg, Sodium 1 mg

Pico de Gallo

Here's the traditional version of this salsa made with tomatoes. If chipotles are difficult to find, you can substitute pequin quebrados or fresh jalapeños, but the smoky, rich flavor of the chipotles will definitely be missed. This is a "Sunday Best" recipe.

PREPARATION TIME: 10 minutes
YIELD: about 2 cups, or 4 servings

    2   dried chipotle chiles, reconstituted (see page 59), or 1 teaspoon chipotle powder
    1   cup diced red, ripe tomato (1 large or 2 or 3 small tomatoes)
    1   cup chopped onion (1 large onion)
    2   cloves garlic, minced
  1/4   cup coarsely chopped cilantro
    2   Tablespoons freshly squeezed lime juice (1 lime)

In a bowl combine the chiles and juice, tomato, onion, garlic, cilantro, and lime juice. Set aside for 5 to 10 minutes for the flavors to blend.

PER SERVING: Calories 30, Protein 1 g, Carbohydrates 7 g, Fiber 1 g, Fat 0 g, Saturated Fat 0 g, Cholesterol 0 mg, Sodium 6 mg

Fruited Salsa

This salsa is especially good served over Grilled Veal Chops (recipe on page 31). You can also serve it over poultry, ham, pork, or fish. With Tortilla Toasts (recipe on page 6), it is good as an appetizer.

PREPARATION TIME: 5 to 7 minutes
YIELD: 4 servings

   2 large, ripe peaches, peeled and chopped
1/2 cup chopped red onion
1/4 cup crushed red caribe chile
   2 Tablespoons lemon juice
1/4 cup coarsely chopped flat-leaf parsley or cilantro

In a bowl combine the peaches, onion, chile, lemon juice, and parsley. Taste and adjust the seasonings. Allow to stand for at least 5 minutes before serving.

PER SERVING: Calories 62, Protein 2 g, Carbohydrates 14 g, Fiber 4 g, Fat 1 g, Saturated Fat 0 g, Cholesterol 0 mg, Sodium 9 mg (Analyzed with cilantro.)

Black-Eyed Pea Salsa

The traditional good-luck pea of the South, black-eyed peas in this salsa are wonderful with pork. The salsa is especially good with Chile Sage Pork Chops (recipe on page 29).

PREPARATION TIME: 5 minutes
YIELD: 4 servings

    2   cups cooked black-eyed peas or 1 (15-ounce) can, drained
  1/2   cup chopped white onion
    2   cloves garlic, minced
  1/3   cup chopped pickled jalapeño chile

In a bowl combine the peas, onion, garlic, and jalapeños. Allow to stand for about 5 minutes before serving.

PER SERVING: Calories 88, Protein 3 g, Carbohydrates 19 g, Fiber 5, Fat 0 g, Saturated Fat 0 g, Cholesterol 0 mg, Sodium 233 mg

White Bean Salsa

White beans—including cannellini, navy, or pea beans—go well in this salsa. It is particularly wonderful with Lamb Chops with Jalapeño Jelly (recipe on page 33). This is a "Sunday Best" recipe.

PREPARATION TIME: 5 minutes
YIELD: 4 servings

- 1 (15-ounce) can white beans, drained
- 2 cloves garlic, minced
- 4 scallions, tender green tops included, thinly sliced
- 2 Tablespoons white wine vinegar
- 2 Tablespoons extra-virgin olive oil, preferably Spanish
- 1/4 cup coarsely chopped cilantro

In a bowl combine the beans, garlic, scallions, vinegar, oil, and cilantro. Allow to stand for at least 10 minutes before serving.

PER SERVING: Calories 191, Protein 9 g, Carbohydrates 24 g, Fiber 6 g, Fat 7 g, Saturated Fat 1 g, Cholesterol 0 mg, Sodium 220 mg

Zippy Glaze

This glaze is almost too good to believe. I like it with honey as well as molasses for glazing roasted, grilled, or broiled poultry or pork.

PREPARATION TIME: 3 to 5 minutes
YIELD: 1 cup*

1/2 cup fragrant-blossom honey, preferably desert honey, such as cactus or mesquite
1 Tablespoon crushed red caribe chile
1/2 cup freshly squeezed orange juice
1 Tablespoon orange zest, optional

In a bowl combine the honey, chile, juice, and zest (if using).

VARIATION: Use molasses instead of honey for a delicious glaze for pork chops.

* This recipe makes enough for 2 pork tenderloins, 3 or 4 large chicken breasts, or 12 chicken thighs

PER SERVING (1/4 recipe): Calories 74, Protein 0 g, Carbohydrates 19 g, Fiber 0 g, Fat 0 g, Saturated Fat 0 g, Cholesterol 0 mg, Sodium 2 mg

Basic Rub

Rubs have long been popular in the Southwest for applying to meats before grilling or roasting. There are many variations; however, I think it's hard to improve on this basic recipe. You can alter the ingredients to please your palate. Make lots; it freezes well and is convenient to have on hand for quick meals. When using, place some of the rub in a shallow bowl and spoon it onto meat or vegetables. Then rub it in. Rub off any excess with a paper towel.

PREPARATION TIME: 3 to 5 minutes
YIELD: 1 3/4 cups

1/2 cup salt
1/2 cup freshly ground black pepper
1/2 cup ground pure mild red chile
  2 Tablespoons garlic granules
  2 Tablespoons sugar

Combine the salt, pepper, chile, garlic, and sugar in a jar. Freeze until ready to use.

PER SERVING (1 Tablespoon): Calories 15, Protein 1 g, Carbohydrates 3 g, Fiber 1 g, Fat 0 g, Saturated Fat 0 g, Cholesterol 0 mg, Sodium 1,996 mg (Note: The salt supplies 100 percent of the sodium; you can use a salt substitute.)

Hot Honey

Hot honey, which became popular in New Mexico a few years ago, is good on meats, in marinades and salad dressings, on corn bread, and anywhere else you like honey.

PREPARATION TIME: 3 minutes
YIELD: 1 cup

    2 Tablespoons ground pure hot chile
    1 cup desert-blossom honey or any good-quality honey

In a 4-cup liquid measuring cup, combine the chiles and honey. Warm for about a minute in the microwave oven.* Stir and allow to cool, then transfer to a jar and keep for later use.

* If you do not have a microwave oven, combine the ingredients in a jar and place in the sun for a week, or heat the mixture in a heavy saucepan over medium-low heat for 5 minutes.

How Sweet It Is . . . Desserts

Most traditional desserts in Southwestern cooking are simple and are patterned after Spanish customs. It was the Spanish who brought sugar, wheat flour, and pork to the Southwest and forever influenced the patterns of the regional desserts.

Now innovation runs high. Many desserts feature traditional ingredients such as chocolate, discovered by the Aztecs, in new, innovative dishes or are used in fanciful renditions of traditional dishes such as tamales. An example is the Hot Fudge Taco I served in my New York City restaurant featuring a sugar cone U-shaped taco shell filled with ice cream and topped with Mexican Hot Fudge Sauce (recipe on page 186).

For this chapter I have combined both trends—traditional and innovative ingredients—to develop light, simple, and flavorful desserts that are quick to make.

A few desserts, such as Margarita Cake (recipe on page 189), require more than five ingredients. But each of the recipes takes twenty minutes or less to make.

*A "Sunday Best" recipe with more than five ingredients but fewer than ten.

Caliente Manzanos

We used to make these when my daughter was a toddler; we called them Amy's Apples. We made them without chile then; instead, we just put the red hots in the hollowed center of each raw apple and frequently topped the apples with marshmallows. Here, the chile adds a spicy note. Frozen yogurt is a wonderful contrast to the hot chiles.

COOKING TIME: 2 1/2 to 3 minutes in a microwave oven, 1 hour in a conventional oven
YIELD: 4 servings

- 4 **baking apples**
- 4 **ounces (1/2 cup) red-hot candies**
- 2 **teaspoons crushed red pequin quebrado chiles**
  Frozen yogurt, vanilla or butter pecan, optional

Wash the apples, then core, removing the entire seed sack. In a small bowl combine the red hots and chiles; stuff into the middle of each apple. To microwave, place each apple in a wineglass.* Cover with plastic wrap and cook one at a time, according to the manufacturer's directions. Serve as is or with a scoop of frozen yogurt.

* Use a simple, everyday wineglass—not a carved or leaded glass—in the microwave.

NOTE: To bake conventionally, stuff the apples and place them in a buttered baking pan. Bake, uncovered, at 375°F (190°C) for 1 hour.

PER SERVING (1 apple): Calories 194, Protein 1 g, Carbohydrates 50 g, Fiber 4 g, Fat 1 g, Saturated Fat 0 g, Cholesterol 0 mg, Sodium 11 mg (Analyzed without frozen yogurt.)

Poached Pears and Pineapple

This simple dish is best if made with Mexican canela, cinnamon that is superior to what is usually found in supermarkets. This is a "Sunday Best" recipe.

COOKING TIME: 5 minutes in a microwave oven, 45 minutes in a conventional oven
YIELD: 4 servings

- 1/2 teaspoon unsalted butter
- 2 pears, peeled, cored, and cut in half lengthwise
- 1/2 cup fresh pineapple chunks or canned slices or wedges
- 1 stick canela or cinnamon, broken into pieces
- 2 Tablespoons honey
- 1/2 cup Cabernet Sauvignon
  Asadero or Brie cheese and water wafers or Tuilles for accompaniment, optional

Butter a glass pie plate or casserole. Place the pear halves around the edge of the plate and the pineapple in the center. Crumble the canela over the top.

In a small bowl combine the honey (warming it first if firm) and wine and pour over all. Cover with plastic wrap and process in the microwave oven at full power for 3 minutes.* Remove from the oven, gently stir the juices (without disturbing the fruit), and spoon the juices over the fruit. Cover and cook for another 2 minutes. Serve warm in a compote glass with the cheese and water wafers, if desired.

* Or bake conventionally, uncovered, in a 375°F (190°C) oven for 45 minutes.

PER SERVING: Calories 116, Protein 1 g, Carbohydrates 24 g, Fiber 2 g, Fat 1 g, Saturated Fat 0 g, Cholesterol 1 mg, Sodium 8 mg

Fruity Tortilla Pizza

When I thought of making a dessert pizza from a flour tortilla, I wondered why the idea hadn't occurred to me before. It is so quick and easy. Now with so many flavored flour tortillas, you can try a "desserty" one, such as apple cinnamon.

COOKING TIME: 5 minutes
YIELD: 4 servings

   1 (12-inch) flour tortilla
   1 cup shredded Monterey Jack cheese or 1/2 cup each cream cheese and shredded Monterey Jack,* divided
   1 cup fresh strawberries or 2 peaches or nectarines, peeled, pitted, and sliced
1/2 cup white seedless grapes or 2 or 3 kiwis, peeled and sliced
   2 Tablespoons fragrant honey
      Several shakes of ground cinnamon

Preheat the oven to 425°F (220°C). Place the tortilla on a baking sheet and sprinkle with about two-thirds of the shredded cheese. Rinse the berries and pat dry. Remove the green stem and any bad spots. Arrange them, pointed tips up, in a circle about 1 inch in from the edge of the tortilla.

Halve the grapes or slice the kiwis. Arrange in circles in the center. Drizzle with the honey, then sprinkle with the remaining cheese. Shake cinnamon over all and bake for 5 minutes or until the cheese melts. Serve warm.

* If using a combination of cheeses, spread the cream cheese on the tortilla and sprinkle the Jack cheese over the fruit.

PER SERVING: Calories 209, Protein 9 g, Carbohydrates 23 g, Fiber 2 g, Fat 10 g, Saturated Fat 6 g, Cholesterol 25 mg, Sodium 220 mg

Fruta Fresca Nachos

Why not make nachos with fresh fruit salsa on a mild cream cheese base? They're delicious and quick and easy to prepare. In fact, you can pass the toppings and let your guests make their own nachos. Select fruits of different colors, such as strawberries, peeled kiwi, and banana or watermelon, honeydew, and banana, or other favorites.

PREPARATION TIME: About 15 minutes
YIELD: 4 servings

     4 (10-inch) flour tortillas
     2 Tablespoons sugar
   1/2 teaspoon ground cinnamon
     2 cups mixed fruit cut into 1/2-inch dice
     1 (3-ounce) package nonfat cream cheese, softened
1 to 2 Tablespoons Triple Sec, optional

Preheat the broiler. Slice each tortilla into 8 pie-shaped wedges. Combine the sugar and cinnamon in a shallow bowl. Quickly dip the tortilla wedges in water, drain briefly on paper toweling or a clean dishcloth, and dip one side in the cinnamon sugar. Arrange on a baking sheet without overlapping. Broil for 2 to 3 minutes, until toasted; let cool.

Place the fruit in a serving bowl and stir well to combine. In another serving bowl combine the cheese with the Triple Sec, if using. Serve a plate of the cinnamon crisps and the bowls of fruit and cheese or, just before serving, spread the cheese on each cinnamon crisp and top with the fruit.

PER SERVING: Calories 315, Protein 10 g, Carbohydrates 56 g, Fiber 4 g, Fat 6 g, Saturated Fat 1 g, Cholesterol 2 g, Sodium 462 mg (Analyzed with watermelon, strawberries, and grapes.)

Berry Blast

The berry flavor blasts through this flavorful cobbler. You'll find yourself making this dessert often, even for company. It is quick to prepare and fun to eat. This is a "Sunday Best" recipe.

BAKING TIME: 5 minutes in a microwave oven, 15 to 20 minutes in a conventional oven
YIELD: 4 servings

- 4 cups assorted fresh berries, such as strawberries, raspberries, blueberries, and blackberries (a combination is best)
- 1 lime
- 1/4 cup sugar or honey
- 3/4 cup all-purpose flour
- 3/4 cup wheat flake cereal, crushed
- 2 Tablespoons unsalted butter, melted
- 1/2 teaspoon ground cinnamon
- 1/2 cup apple juice concentrate
  Frozen yogurt or low-fat ice cream, optional

Preheat the oven to 425°F (220°C).* Rinse the berries and place in a buttered baking dish. Squeeze the lime evenly over the top. Sprinkle with the sugar. In a bowl combine the flour, cereal, butter, and cinnamon. Stir in the apple juice. Spread the batter over the berries. Bake for 15 to 20 minutes, until the topping is browned and crusty. Serve with frozen yogurt, if desired.

* To cook in the microwave oven, prepare the dessert as described, cover with wax paper, and cook on high power for 5 minutes or until the crust is crisp. Cook for an additional minute or two, if needed.

PER SERVING: Calories 339, Protein 5 g, Carbohydrates 68 g, Fiber 8 g, Fat 7, Saturated Fat 4 g, Cholesterol 16 mg, Sodium 63 mg

Spicy Broiled Pineapple

Pineapple takes well to grilling. The firm texture and sweet taste are accented by the hot chiles and sweet honey.

COOKING TIME: 4 to 6 minutes in a microwave oven, 5 to 8 minutes under the broiler or on the grill
YIELD: 4 servings

- 1 small, ripe pineapple or 1 (14 1/2-ounce) can pineapple rings
- 3 Tablespoons dark, flavorful, blossom honey or Hot Honey (recipe on page 174)
- 1/2 teaspoon ground hot red chile such as pequin or cayenne or to taste
- 2 Tablespoons dark rum

To prepare the pineapple, hold it upright and slice vertically through the green top and down through the fruit, leaving the top attached to the pineapple. Cut the pineapple into quarters by slicing each half through the top. Cut off the rind and cut into bite-size pieces, leaving the pieces intact on top of the rind.

Place each quarter pineapple, cut side up, in a microwavable baking dish.* In a small bowl mix the honey and chile and spread on the pineapple. Drizzle with the rum. Cook in the microwave oven on full power for 4 to 6 minutes, until hot. Serve with the green top still attached. Spoon the honey mixture over the top.

* If grilling the pineapple, place each quarter on a baking sheet, drizzle with the honey mixture and rum, then transfer to the grill. If broiling, leave the pineapple on the baking sheet and broil for 5 to 8 minutes, until browned on the edges and hot throughout.

PER SERVING: Calories 122, Protein 1 g, Carbohydrates 28 g, Fiber 2 g, Fat 1 g, Saturated Fat 0 g, Cholesterol 0 mg, Sodium 2 mg

Deep Summer's Delight—Watermelon Freeze

Make this when you have fifteen minutes or so early in the day. You can even make it a few days ahead. It takes about an hour or so to set up firmly. It is a refreshing finish to barbecued or grilled dinners of any sort. Crisp cookies complement the fruity flavor of this dessert.

PREPARATION TIME: 15 minutes
YIELD: 4 servings

  2 pounds seedless watermelon
  1/2 cup pineapple juice
  1/4 cup Triple Sec, peach schnapps, or other fruity liqueur
      Crisp cookies, optional

Remove the rind and cut the watermelon into about 1-inch cubes. Pour the juice and liqueur into a blender. Add the watermelon and process until pureed. Spoon the mixture into wine glasses or a freezable shallow container. Freeze for at least 1 hour before serving. Serve with crisp cookies, if desired.

PER SERVING: Calories 135, Protein 1 g, Carbohydrates 33 g, Fiber 2 g, Fat 0 g, Saturated Fat 0 g, Cholesterol 0 mg, Sodium 9 mg

Berry Brûlée

This wonderful, low-fat version of the ever-popular French dessert takes on a Spanish flair with fresh fruit and low-fat ingredients. Try this dessert when you feel like splurging but without a lot of calories. This is a "Sunday Best" recipe.

COOKING TIME: 20 minutes
YIELD: 4 servings

1	pint fresh berries such as strawberries, raspberries, or blueberries
1/4	cup sugar, divided
1	Tablespoon cornstarch
1 1/4	cups evaporated skim milk or regular skim milk
1	large egg, beaten
1/2	teaspoon Mexican vanilla extract

Portion the berries among 4 small, buttered ovenproof serving bowls.

Reserve 4 teaspoons of the sugar and set aside. In a heavy, 3-quart saucepan, combine the remaining sugar and the cornstarch. Stir in the milk and egg. Place over medium-high heat. As soon as tiny bubbles start to form, reduce the heat to low and cook until the mixture thickens, stirring constantly.

Remove from the heat and beat to hasten cooling. Stir in the vanilla. Divide the mixture among the bowls, spooning it evenly over the berries. Place in the refrigerator until serving time. Place the bowls on a baking sheet and sprinkle each with 1 teaspoon of the reserved sugar. Place under the broiler until the sugar browns. Serve immediately.

PER SERVING: Calories 160, Protein 8 g, Carbohydrates 29g, Fiber 2 g, Fat 2 g, Saturated Fat 1 g, Cholesterol 56 mg, Sodium 109 mg

Mexican Cinnamon Chocolate Roll-Ups

The Aztecs, who discovered chocolate, thought that chocolate should always be paired with cinnamon—a delightful combination. Even Mexican bar chocolate has cinnamon in it.

PREPARATION TIME: 3 to 5 minutes
YIELD: 4 servings

- 1 pint low-fat ice cream or frozen yogurt, vanilla, chocolate, or caramel
- 4 chocolate-flavored flour tortillas*
- 1/4 cup Mexican Hot Fudge Sauce (recipe on page 186), or any favorite kind with a generous pinch of ground cinnamon stirred in
  Cocoa and ground cinnamon, to sprinkle on plate

Place scoops of ice cream on each tortilla, roll up, and place seam side down on 4 dessert plates. Warm the fudge sauce for 15 to 30 seconds in the microwave oven or over hot water. Belt the sauce over the center of the filled tortilla. Holding your hand about a foot above the plates, let a pinch of cocoa drift onto the rim of each. Repeat with the cinnamon. Serve immediately.

* Chocolate and other flavored tortillas are becoming increasingly popular. Note the online order sources (page 209) if you'd like to order them.

PER SERVING: Calories 414, Protein 12 g, Carbohydrates 72 g, Fiber 3, Fat 10 g, Saturated Fat 3 g, Cholesterol 8 mg, Sodium 431 mg (Analyzed with low-fat ice cream.)
PER SERVING: Calories 342, Protein 12 g, Carbohydrates 61g, Fiber 3 g, Fat 6 g, Saturated Fat 1 g, Cholesterol 2 mg, Sodium 414 mg (Analyzed with nonfat frozen yogurt.)

Mexican Hot Fudge Sauce

This sauce is so easy to make. Mexican bar chocolate contains sweeteners, cinnamon, and other spices. This sauce keeps well in the freezer.

PREPARATION TIME: 10 minutes
YIELD: 1/2 cup

 2 ounces (2 squares) Mexican chocolate*
1/2 cup evaporated milk or evaporated skim milk
1/4 teaspoon Mexican vanilla extract

Coarsely chop the chocolate and place in a heavy, 3-quart saucepan. Add the milk and vanilla and cook on medium to low heat, stirring, for about 10 minutes, or until all the chocolate is melted, well mixed, and thickened.

* If Mexican chocolate is not available, use sweetened baking chocolate and add 1/4 teaspoon each ground cinnamon, nutmeg, and cloves.

PER SERVING (1 Tablespoon): Calories 34, Protein 1 g, Carbohydrates 6 g, Fiber 0 g, Fat 1 g, Saturated Fat 0 g, Cholesterol 1 mg, Sodium 19 mg (Analyzed using evaporated skim milk.)

Spicy Hot Chocolate Mousse

As rich as mousse tastes, it is surprisingly easy to make. High-quality chocolate is a must; bittersweet chocolate is preferred. The unexpected heat of this dessert comes from the spicy, red-hot cinnamon schnapps.

COOKING TIME: 10 minutes
YIELD: 4 servings

- 1/2 **cup sugar, divided**
- 4 **ounces (4 squares) high-quality bittersweet baking chocolate**
- 2 **Tablespoons unsalted butter, cut into small bits**
- 1 **Tablespoon red-hot schnapps or to taste**
- 3 **large egg whites**

In a liquid measuring cup, combine 1/4 cup water and 1/4 cup of the sugar. Microwave for 1 minute on full power to dissolve the sugar, or on a conventional range, bring to a boil in a small saucepan and cook until dissolved.

In a heavy saucepan or a double boiler over medium-low heat, combine the chocolate and butter, whisking continuously until melted and of a creamy texture. Whisk or mix in the schnapps and 2 Tablespoons of the sugar mixture. Taste and add the remaining sugar mixture, if desired.

Place the egg whites in a mixing bowl. Using clean beaters for the electric mixer, beat until foamy. Sprinkle the remaining 1/4 cup sugar evenly over the top. Beat on high speed to create a soft meringue. Fold the meringue into the chocolate mixture. Serve warm or chilled in footed compotes or wineglasses.

PER SERVING: Calories 330, Protein 5 g, Carbohydrates 43 g, Fiber 2 g, Fat 15 g, Saturated Fat 9 g, Cholesterol 17 mg, Sodium 44 mg

Sweet Potato or Pumpkin Pudding

This dessert is most easily made with canned pumpkin; however, if you prefer the taste of sweet potatoes, just puree a 15-ounce can drained sweet potatoes or bake or stew 1 1/2 pounds of fresh sweet potatoes until done.

PREPARATION TIME: 5 to 7 minutes in a microwave oven, 30 to 40 minutes in a conventional oven

YIELD: 6 to 8 servings

> 2 cups pureed sweet potato or pumpkin or 1 (15-ounce) can
> 1 1/2 cups evaporated skim milk
> 1 large egg, plus 1 large egg white
> 1/2 cup firmly packed light-brown sugar
> 2 teaspoons pumpkin pie spice or 1/4 teaspoon each ground ginger, nutmeg, allspice, and cloves

In a blender combine the sweet potato, milk, egg and egg white, brown sugar, and spice. Process to blend well. Pour the mixture into 6 to 8 individual buttered baking dishes. Place in the microwave oven and cook on high for 5 minutes,* or until a table knife inserted in the center comes out clean. Cook for another minute or 2, if needed. Serve warm.

* Or preheat a conventional oven to 350°F (180°C). Place the pudding dishes in a baking pan large enough to hold them. Add hot water to about halfway up the sides of the baking dishes. Place the pan in the oven and bake for 30 to 40 minutes, until a knife inserted in the center comes out clean.

PER SERVING (1/8 recipe): Calories 167, Protein 6 g, Carbohydrates 34 g, Fiber 2 g, Fat 1 g, Saturated Fat 0 g, Cholesterol 28 mg, Sodium 124 mg (Analyzed with sweet potatoes.)

PER SERVING (1/8 recipe): Calories 157, Protein 5g, Carbohydrates 33 g, Fiber 4 g, Fat 1 g, Saturated Fat 0 g, Cholesterol 28 mg, Sodium 186 mg (Analyzed with pumpkin.)

Margarita Cake

This delicious cake is a fun dessert for an impromptu dinner party. And it is low in calories. You can vary the liquors; rum or bourbon would give it an entirely different flavor. This is a "Sunday Best" recipe.

BAKING TIME: 20 minutes
YIELD: 8 servings

1	large orange
1 1/4	cups sugar
3	Tablespoons tequila, silver or gold
2	large eggs
1/4	cup skim milk
3/4	cup all-purpose flour
1 1/2	teaspoons baking powder
1/4	cup butter, melted
	Powdered sugar for garnish, optional
	Orange twists for garnish, optional*

Preheat the oven to 375°F (190°C). Butter a springform pan, or line an 8-inch round pan with wax paper. Use a zester to remove as much zest as possible from the orange, then halve the orange and juice it. Measure the juice, adding water to make 1/2 cup. Combine the orange juice, zest, and sugar in a small pan. Bring to a boil to dissolve the sugar, then remove from the heat. When cool, add the tequila. Reserve this syrup to use over the cake when done. Do not add to the batter.

In a food processor or blender, combine the eggs, milk, flour, baking powder, and butter. Process until the ingredients are combined, scraping down the sides of the container. Place the batter in the prepared pan and bake for 20 minutes, or until the cake pulls away from the sides of the pan and springs back when touched with a finger.

If using a springform pan, place the cake, still in the pan, on a plate to catch the drips. Otherwise, transfer the cake from the pan to a plate 15 minutes after it comes out of the oven. Pierce the top of the cake with a fork in several places, then slowly drizzle the tequila syrup over the cake. Remove the springform pan sides, but not the bottom. Sprinkle the cake with the powdered sugar and decorate with orange twists, if desired.

* To make orange twists, cut an orange in half, then thinly slice each half to the rind and twist. Twist the ends of each slice in opposite directions.

PER SERVING: Calories 255, Protein 3, Carbohydrates 42 g, Fiber 0 g, Fat 7 g, Saturated Fat 4 g, Cholesterol 70 mg, Sodium 122 mg

Banana Oatmeal Cookies

Banana and apple juice reduce the need for much fat in these cookies. They stay moist if well sealed and are a delicious, healthy snack. Freeze them if keeping more than three to five days. This is a "Sunday Best" recipe.

BAKING TIME: 10 to 12 minutes
YIELD: 36 cookies

	Nonstick oil spray
3/4	cup mashed banana (3 small bananas)
1/4	cup vegetable oil
1	(12-ounce) can apple juice concentrate
2	teaspoons pure vanilla extract
3	cups whole-wheat or all-purpose flour
1 1/4	cups dry oatmeal, any kind
1	teaspoon baking soda

Preheat the oven to 375°F (190°C). Spray 2 baking sheets with nonstick oil spray. In a mixing bowl or food processor, combine the banana, oil, juice, and vanilla.

In another bowl combine the flour, oatmeal, and baking soda. Add to the banana mixture and combine until well blended. Drop by spoonful onto the prepared baking sheets, leaving about 2 inches between each. Bake for 10 to 12 minutes, until firm when pressed with a finger. Transfer to cooling racks.

PER SERVING (1 cookie): Calories 82, Protein 2 g, Carbohydrates 15 g, Fiber 2 g, Fat 2 g, Saturated Fat 0 g, Cholesterol 0 mg, Sodium 39 mg

Quick Low-Fat Brownies

These brownies are so quick and low in calories that I had to include this recipe. This is a "Sunday Best" recipe.

BAKING TIME: 20 to 25 minutes
YIELD: 16 brownies

  1/2 cup all-purpose flour
  1/2 cup unsweetened cocoa
      Pinch of salt
    2 large egg whites
    1 large egg
  3/4 cup sugar
  1/3 cup unsweetened applesauce
    2 Tablespoons vegetable oil
    2 teaspoons pure vanilla extract

Preheat the oven to 375°F (190°C). Generously butter or spray an 8 x 8-inch baking pan. In a small bowl combine the flour, cocoa, and salt.

In a large bowl combine the egg whites, egg, sugar, applesauce, oil, and vanilla. Mix in the flour mixture, then pour into the prepared pan. Sprinkle the top with nuts, if desired. Bake for 20 minutes, then check for doneness. The brownies should spring back when pressed with a finger or an inserted toothpick comes out clean. Place on a cooling rack for 10 minutes, then invert the pan. Let stand until cool to the touch, then cut into sixteen 2-inch pieces.

VARIATION: Spread this simple chocolate glaze over the brownies for additional flavor. In a small pan heat 2 squares semisweet chocolate and 1 Tablespoon unsalted butter. Remove from the heat and whisk in 1/2 cup powdered sugar. Mix in 2 to 3 Tablespoons milk to reach the desired consistency. Glaze the brownies after they cool. Scatter with 2 Tablespoons chopped nuts, if desired.

PER SERVING (1 brownie without nuts): Calories 83, Protein 2 g, Carbohydrates 15 g, Fiber 1 g, Fat 2 g, Saturated Fat 1 g, Cholesterol 13 mg, Sodium 12 mg

*A "Sunday Best" recipe with more than five ingredients but fewer than ten.

Beverages—to Sip and Cool Off With

The most popular drink before a Southwestern or Mexican meal is a margarita, which is now America's favorite drink. However, beer and wine are also popular.

Mexican beer is good and varied. Interestingly, the first beer on the North American continent was made in Mexico by the Germans. This legacy is noteworthy in both the flavor and quality of Mexican beer.

Wine goes well with spicy foods. Many people prefer to complement the spiciness with sweet white wines, such as Gerwürztraminer, and hearty red wines, such as Zinfandel. The choices are personal; I prefer drier wines almost consistently.

Following are several of my favorite mixed drinks that are particularly good before Southwestern brunches, lunches, and dinners. I've also included Mexican Orange Vanilla Water (recipe on page 195), a nonalcoholic drink.

Margaritas

Now America's favorite mixed drink, margaritas can be made in numerous ways. Nothing, however, is better than the original margarita made with quality ingredients. The origin of the margarita is a bit fuzzy; most people seem to agree that the first one was named for a beautiful woman named Margaret. A man at a bar in a Mexican village, some say San Miguel de Allende, couldn't take his eyes off the woman. He was drinking shooters of tequila with fresh lime and salt. The bartender helped him out by making his drinks for him, squeezing fresh lime juice into a salt-rimmed glass and adding tequila.

Years ago, our backyard neighbor in Albuquerque, Bob Tolliver, began calling my Perfect Margaritas, made with three parts tequila, "crawl home margaritas" and the tamer ones, made with two parts tequila, "walk home margaritas." The names stuck; I even tell the story in my cooking classes. My favorite recipe follows. I prefer them made with the optional egg white.

YIELD: 4 to 6 servings

1/2	cup freshly squeezed lime juice (about 4 limes)
1/2	cup Triple Sec or orange liqueur
1	cup tequila, silver or clear*
1	teaspoon fresh egg white—preferably pasteurized, optional
	Salt or sugar, for edging the glass

Place the lime juice, Triple Sec, and tequila in a blender with a few ice cubes. Add the egg white, if using, and process until well mixed and frothy. Pour into a chilled glass edged with salt or sugar** and containing 4 or 5 ice cubes.

* You may prefer the stronger flavor of gold tequila. And instead of Triple Sec, you can substitute Cointreau, Curacao, or Grand Marnier. For the stronger "crawl home margaritas," which I call Perfect Margaritas, increase the amount of tequila to 1 1/2 cups.

** An hour or so before serving, rub a lime rind (left from squeezing the juice) around the rim of footed or high ball glasses. Gently dip the rim in salt or sugar and place the glasses in the freezer.

FRUIT VARIATIONS: For other fruit flavors, cut fruit such as watermelon, raspberries strawberries, or pineapple into chunks and place in a liquid measuring cup, not exceeding 1/2 cup. Another popular fruit is agave juice. Tamarind pods can be cut in half and the pulp scraped into a measuring cup. Pour lime juice over the fruit to the 1/2-cup measure. The juice will fill in the nooks and crannies and always seems to be just the right blend of lime to fruit. Frozen fruits can be used.

PER SERVING (1/6 recipe): Calories 162, Protein 0 g, Carbohydrates 11 g, Fiber 0 g, Fat 0 g, Saturated Fat 0 g, Cholesterol 0 mg, Sodium 2 mg, (Analyzed without salt, sugar, or egg white.)

Mexican Orange Vanilla Water

We serve pitchers of this refreshing water to our students at the cooking school and get lots of compliments.

YIELD: 4 servings

1/2	seedless navel orange
1-inch	piece Mexican vanilla bean*
32	ounces water

Cut the orange into 1/4-inch slices and place them and the vanilla in a pitcher of water. Refrigerate for an hour or so before serving.

* You can refill the pitcher a time or two and recycle the vanilla bean two or three times, adding fresh orange slices each time.

Frank and Diane's Margarita Punch

Frank Vertucca and Diane Gedymin are a publishing couple—Frank in sales and Diane in editing. I met them at the Rocky Mountain Book Fair a few years ago, and they shared this recipe with me.

YIELD: 4 to 6 servings

  1 (6-ounce) can frozen limeade
  1 (12-ounce) can good-quality beer
  6 ounces tequila gold
  3 ounces Triple Sec
  1 large egg white

In a blender combine the limeade, beer, tequila, Triple Sec, egg white, and several ice cubes or chunks. Process until well mixed and frothy. Chill in the refrigerator or over ice in a punch bowl or pitcher. Serve in salt- or sugar-rimmed glasses with ice (see page 194).

PER SERVING (1/6 recipe): Calories 212, Protein 1 g, Carbohydrates 27 g, Fiber 0 g, Fat 0 g, Saturated Fat 0 g, Cholesterol 0 mg, Sodium 13 mg

Easy Margarita Punch

This punch is simpler and easier to make than standard margaritas.

YIELD: 4 to 6 servings

1   (12-ounce) can frozen limeade
12   ounces silver tequila
1/2   cup Triple Sec, optional

Combine the limeade, tequila, Triple Sec (if using), and several ice cubes or chunks. Mix with a spoon or whisk. Chill in the refrigerator or over ice and serve in salt- or sugar-rimmed glasses over ice (see page 194).

VARIATION: I frequently make this without Triple Sec because the limeade is sweet enough. For virgin margaritas, use 12 ounces sparkling water, ginger ale, 7 Up or similar lime-lemon carbonated drink, and 1/2 cup orange juice instead of tequila and Triple Sec.

PER SERVING (1/6 recipe): Calories 265, Protein 0 g, Carbohydrates 36 g, Fiber 0 g, Fat 0 g, Saturated Fat 0 g, Cholesterol 0 mg, Sodium 1 mg (Analyzed without Triple Sec.)
PER SERVING (1/6 recipe): Calories 335, Protein 0 g, Carbohydrates 45 g, Fiber 0 g, Fat 0 g, Saturated Fat 0 g, Cholesterol 0 mg, Sodium 2 mg (Analyzed with Triple Sec.)

Sangria, New Mexican Style

This sangria is much lighter than some versions made with brandies and stronger liquor combinations. This is a "Sunday Best" recipe.

YIELD: 4 to 6 servings

1/2 cup sugar
1/2 cup water
  1 stick cinnamon or canela
  3 limes, 2 juiced and 1 sliced
  1 orange, sliced
  1 bottle (750 ml or a fifth) hearty red wine, such as Zinfandel or Cabernet

In a saucepan combine the sugar, water, and cinnamon stick. Bring to a boil and cook only until the sugar dissolves. This can be done days ahead.

Remove the cinnamon stick from the sugar syrup. Combine the syrup with the lime juice, lime slices, orange slices, and wine. Mix to combine well. Serve over ice in stemmed or tall glasses.

PER SERVING (1/6 recipe): Calories 157, Protein 0 g, Carbohydrates 20 g, Fiber 0 g, Fat 0 g, Saturated Fat 0 g, Cholesterol 0 mg, Sodium 7 mg (Analyzed without garnish.)

Randy's Ramos Gin Fizzes

Randy, a dear friend of ours who lived in the Phoenix area, made these for us one weekend morning when we were visiting. More than thirty years later, we still have not found a gin fizz that tastes as good. We always serve them on New Year's Day morning. They are wonderful preceding a brunch. Although these fizzes were originally made with gin, you can substitute vodka or tequila. This is a "Sunday Best" recipe.

YIELD: 4 servings

- 1/4 cup orange juice concentrate
- 1 Tablespoon freshly squeezed lemon juice (about 1/2 lemon)
- 1/4 cup vodka, gin, or tequila
- 3/4 cup skim or whole milk
- 1 large egg white
- 1 Tablespoon plus 2 teaspoons sugar

Place the orange juice, lemon juice, and vodka in a blender. Add 4 ice cubes and process until well mixed. Add the milk, egg white, and sugar; blend until frothy and smooth and the ice is well chipped. Serve in stemmed glasses.

PER SERVING: Calories 102, Protein 3 g, Carbohydrates 15 g, Fiber 0 g, Fat 0 g, Saturated Fat 0 g, Cholesterol 1 mg, Sodium 38 mg

Daiquiris

Daiquiris used to be much more popular than they are today. They make up well in large quantities for entertaining and can be varied to use almost any fruit you have on hand. When we lived in Albuquerque in the 1960s and had an apricot tree we loved making apricot daiquiris.

YIELD: 4 servings

1 (6-ounce) can frozen limeade
6 ounces light rum

Place the limeade and rum in a blender, add several ice cubes, and process until slushy. Serve.

VARIATION: For a fruity variation, use 3 ounces frozen limeade and 1/2 cup chopped fruit such as apricots, bananas, and strawberries.

PER SERVING: 198 calories, Protein 0 g, Carbohydrates 27 g, Fiber 0 g, Fat 0 g, Saturated Fat 0 g, Cholesterol 0 mg, Sodium 0 mg

Menus

For quick and easy entertaining or for simple family meals, these recipes can be endlessly combined.

One element is sure. Southwestern cooking is so flavorful and fun that the fiesta fever is sure to make any of your meals wonderfully memorable.

For entertaining, be sure to use bright colors—from hand-painted earthenware pottery to brightly colored table coverings—to set the happy, festive mood that spells Southwestern dining. Mariachi (Mexican street band) music is always appropriate. Brightly colored flowers or cacti can make attractive centerpieces. Of course, low arrangements, about 6 inches high, are best for seated dinners.

New Year's Eve Party

Hot Chile Almonds (recipe on page 15)
Assorted Quesadillas with Salsas (recipe on page 16 and 158–171)
Oaxacan Gorditos (recipe on page 128)
Fajita bar with Pico de Gallo (recipes on pages 138 and 168)
Spicy Hot Chocolate Mousse (recipe on page 187)
Poached Pears and Pineapple (recipe on page 178)

You can ready this party easily with a little advance preparation. Prepare the Hot Chile Almonds several days ahead, even before the holidays. Prepare the salsas a day ahead. Sauté the chorizo and chipotles for the gorditos. Marinate the meat for the fajitas, making at least two kinds, such as chicken and beef, if the party is large. Prepare the desserts a day ahead. A few hours ahead, grill the quesadillas and roll the gorditos; keep them in a warm oven. Present the quesadillas on a large mirror, held up with glass bricks, over votive candles in glass holders. To display the quesadillas, prepare attractive designs with the salsas and confetti sprinkles of chiles and spritzes of flavored sour cream. Present the fajitas and gorditos on a warming tray. Place the desserts on a different table or bring them out later.

Super Bowl Party

Pinto Pate with Tortilla Toasts (recipes on pages 4 and 6)
Chile Cheesed Tortilla Roll-ups with salsa (recipes on pages 10 and 158–171)
Speedy Enchiladas or Speedy Chili with Fixin's 'n Mixin's (recipes on page 125 or 93)
Spinach and Corn Rolled Enchiladas or Turkey Chili with a Margarita Splash (recipes on page 153 or 76)
Quick Low-Fat Brownies (recipe on page 191)

All the recipes here can be made a day ahead so you can have a good time watching the ball game with your guests. Just before they arrive, warm the tortilla roll-ups and display on the salsa. Set out the pate and toasts. Heat the enchiladas or chilis for serving at halftime or when the game is over. If desired, serve warm wheat tortillas for guests to eat as is or to roll around the chili and the Fixin's 'n Mixin's to make burritos. (Fixin's 'n Mixin's are garnishes for the chili. My favorites are coarsely shredded mixed Monterey Jack and Cheddar cheeses, chopped onion, pickled jalapeños, and sour cream with lime wedges edged with mild chile.)

Set out plates of brownies for dessert after the main course is served.

VALENTINE'S DAY DINNER FOR TWO

Blue Corn Tortilla Toasts with Salsa Marinated Mexican "Caviar" (recipe on page 5)

Salsa Snapper Soup (recipe on page 91)

Aztec-Style Pork Chops (recipe on page 30)

Tossed green salad, your favorite

Mexicali Rice Pilaf (recipe on page 108)

Berry Brûlée (recipe on page 184)

To make these dishes for two, you can cut each recipe in half or have an easy dinner a couple of days later. Prepare the toasts several days ahead. Marinate the "caviar" and the pork chops a day ahead. Prepare the brûlées a day or so ahead. Prepare all the ingredients for the pilaf an hour or so ahead. Prepare the soup. To serve, grill the pork chops and keep in a warm oven. Enjoy the "caviar" while the soup is warming and the pilaf is cooking. Serve the soup followed by the pork chops and the pilaf. For a special touch, flame the brûlée by spooning a Tablespoon of raspberry liqueur over each while they are still hot from melting the sugar, then ignite.

NEW MEXICAN SAINT PATRICK'S DAY DINNER

Green Daiquiris (recipe on page 200)

Chevre Wrap with green tortillas (recipe on page 127)

Guacamole with Tortilla Toasts (recipes on pages 3 and 6)

Quick Green Chile Stew (recipe on page 92)

Margarita Cake (recipe on page 189)

Prepare the cake, using two limes instead of an orange, a day ahead. Make the toasts the day before. If desired, prepare the stew a day ahead. If possible, buy the green spinach wheat tortillas; see online order sources (page 209) if not available in your markets. Prepare the Chevre Wrap a day ahead. Just before your guests arrive, prepare the green daiquiris. Serve the daiquiris with the guacamole. When you're ready to serve dinner, warm or prepare the green chile stew. Serve the tortillas warmed with butter on the side. Serve the cake for dessert.

Spring Welcome Brunch

Randy's Ramos Gin Fizzes (recipe on page 199)

Spicy Bacon Bites (recipe on page 9)

Nacho Crisps with Goat Cheese, Fruit, and Lime Salsa (recipe on page 7)

Breakfast Wrap (recipe on page 137)

Crumb-Coated Halibut with Tomatillo Salsa (recipe on pages 87 and 160)

Spicy Broiled Pineapple (recipe on page 182)

The day before, prepare the crumbs for the bacon and halibut. Toast the nacho crisps and prepare the salsa for the nachos. Prepare the Tomatillo Salsa too. Slice the pineapple and cover well. An hour before, measure the ingredients for the drinks. Prepare the halibut so it is ready for baking. Coat the bacon bites and bake just before your guests arrive. Prepare the nachos. Just before serving, prepare the eggs for the wrap and bake the halibut. Broil the pineapple just before you are ready to serve dessert.

Cinco de Mayo Party

Margaritas—many flavors, if desired (recipe on page 194)

Black Bean and Goat Cheese Chalupitas (recipe on page 11)

Stuffed Jalapeños (recipe on page 18)

Quickie Quesos (recipe on page 17)

Flank Steak and/or Soft Chicken Tacos (recipe on page 23 or 70)

Salsas (recipes on pages 158–171)

Snappy Beans 'n Rice (recipe on page 111)

Quick Low-fat Brownies and Banana Oatmeal Cookies (recipe on pages 191 and 190)

The day before, prepare the tortillas for the chalupitas and the quesos. Stuff the jalapeños. Rub the chicken breast (and/or flank steak) for the tacos. Prepare the salsas and make the cookies. Set the table with bright Mexican colors. About an hour before the party, prepare the lime juice and fruit for the margaritas. Grill the flank steak and chicken; cut and keep warm. Prepare the bean dish. Just before your guests arrive, finish the chalupitas and quesos. Serve the dessert on a separate table, if possible.

Summery Southwestern Barbecue

Sangria (recipe on page 198)
Southwestern Barbecue Pizza bites (recipe on page 55)
Grilled Lamb Fajitas with Pico de Gallo (recipes on pages 32 and 168)
Chicken Rice Salad with Jalapeño Lime Creme Dressing (recipes on pages 40 and 48)
Spicy Hot Chocolate Mousse (recipe on page 187)

The day before, prepare the sangria mix, pizza toppings, and tortillas for the pizzas. Marinate the fajitas and make the pico de gallo. Cook the rice for the salad and make the dressing. Prepare the mousse. About an hour before the party, prepare the sangria and compile the pizzas ready for baking. Combine the salad ingredients and set everything out for the party, preferably on a patio or deck.

Fourth of July Fiesta

Grilled Veggie Bites with Spicy Salsa (recipes on pages 13 and 158)
Blue Corn Tortilla Toasts with Salsa Marinated Mexican "Caviar" (recipe on page 5)
Swiss Chard–Wrapped Salmon (recipe on page 133)
Chicken Chile Pasta (recipe on page 58)
Berry Blast with frozen yogurt (recipe on page 181)

This is a red, white, and blue menu. Early in the day or the day before, prepare the salsa, the toasts, and the "caviar." Prepare the salmon and the pasta dish. Prepare the blast (use blueberries and strawberries and serve with vanilla frozen yogurt for a red, white, and blue color scheme) or prepare it for baking and bake just before the guests arrive. Serve the meal outdoors using red, white, and blue table decorations.

Labor Day Lawn Party

Rockefeller Roll-Ups (recipe on page 126)
Calabacita Crisps with salsas (recipes on pages 8 and 158–171)
Chile Rubbed, Grilled Rib Eye Steak or Sweetheart Barbecued Chicken (recipes on pages 22 or 71)
Presto Potato Salad (recipe on page 106)
Deep Summer's Delight—Watermelon Freeze (recipe on page 183)

Prepare the roll-ups, the crisps, and the salsa the day before or early in the day. Rub the steaks or the chicken and make the potato salad. Prepare the Watermelon Freeze. About an hour before your guests arrive, scoop the freeze into small balls and place in brandy or wineglasses to serve (any small stemmed glass will be fine). Just before the guests arrive, set out the two appetizers for guests to enjoy while you grill the steaks or chicken.

All Saints' Day Dinner

This popular Mexican holiday is sometimes called the Day of the Dead. I prefer All Saints' Day. Halloween is celebrated the eve before.

Margaritas (recipe on pages 194)
Scottsdale Toasts with Chile Jack Melt (recipe on page 2)
Shrimp de Ajo with Refried Black Beans (recipe on page 12)
Snapper Sauced in Salsa (recipe on page 86)
Herbed, Quick-Baked Potato Wedges (recipe on page 104)
Tossed green salad, your favorite
Mexican Cinnamon Chocolate Roll-Ups (recipe on page 185)

Ahead of time, squeeze the juice for the margaritas. Prepare the toast for the toasts. Shell and devein the shrimp and marinate them. Prepare the tostado quarters for the shrimp appetizer. Mince the herbs for the potatoes. Prepare the salad, salad dressing (tossing the salad just before serving), and dessert. To serve, top the toasts with the cheese and melt it. Prepare the shrimp appetizers. Place the snapper in a baking dish with the other ingredients. Bake the snapper and potatoes while your guests have appetizers. Toss the salad and serve. For dessert, serve the chocolate roll-ups on the fudge sauce with the plates dusted with cocoa.

Spicy Dinner for a Cold, Chilly Night

Double Corned Fritters with Quick-Smoked Shrimp and Jalapeño
Lime Crème (recipes on pages 19 and 48)
Chile Sage Pork Chops with Black-Eyed Pea Salsa (recipes on pages 29 and 170)
Chipotle and Roasted Garlic Mashed Potatoes (recipe on page 103)
Spinach and Pear Salad with Piñons (recipe on page 41)
Sweet Potato or Pumpkin Pudding (recipe on page 188)

Ahead of time, prepare the fritter batter, smoke the shrimp, and prepare the lime creme. Prepare the sage rub and rub into the chops. Prepare the salsa, chipotles, and salad dressing. (Omit the shrimp in the salad for this menu.) Prepare the pudding. Just before your guests arrive, prepare the fritters and keep warm. Boil the potatoes and preheat the grill, if using. Serve this meal formally, in courses, with the fritters and shrimp first, followed by the pork and potatoes. Serve the salad with the pork or as a course by itself. End with the pudding.

EASY CHRISTMAS EVE PARTY

Guacamole with Tortilla Toasts (recipe on pages 3 and 6)

Shrimp Salad Burrito bites (recipe on page 130)

Cumin Chicken Chimi (recipe on page 135)

Tortilla Pizzas (recipe on page 52)

Grilled Turkey Tenders served with warm corn tortillas (recipe on page 74)

Trio of salsas, your choice (recipes on pages 158–171)

Christmas cookies, candies, and fruitcake

Quick Low-Fat Brownies (recipe on page 191)

A day or two ahead, prepare the Tortilla Toasts and the Mexicali rice for the shrimp burritos. Marinate the chicken for the chimis and bake the tortillas for the pizzas. Marinate the turkey tenders and make the salsas. Decorate the buffet table with festive Christmas colors, emphasizing the red, green, and white of Christmas and the Mexican flag. Arrange the cookies, candies, fruitcake, and brownies on a pretty tray and cover tightly with plastic wrap.

Two hours before the party, make the guacamole, prepare the lettuce for the shrimp burritos, cook the chicken for the chimis, and prepare the toppings for the pizzas. Just before your guests arrive, prepare several pizzas with different toppings; make more during the party if desired. Roll the chimis and burritos, and organize an attractive presentation of the turkey tenders on a large platter. Place all the food on the table, then kick back and enjoy the party.

VEGETARIAN MENUS

To create vegetarian menus, use the vegetarian recipes in the chapter starting on page 141 or those in other chapters, and substitute these dishes in the above menus. Some selections are already vegetarian.

APPENDIX

ONLINE ORDER SOURCES

Southwestern ingredients are increasingly available, although the highest-quality ingredients, such as ground pure chiles, herbs, and corn products, can be hard to find. The following three sources should be able to fill any ingredient needs you may have.

For ground pure chiles, herbs, corn products, and essentials for authentic Southwestern cooking. Or, for special Southwestern cooking gear, ingredients, and Jane Butel's cookbooks:

Pecos Valley Spice Co.
P.O. Box 2162
Corrales, NM 87048
505-243-2622

www.pecosvalleyspice.com

For:
Jane Butel's Cooking School Pantry
125 Second Street NW
Albuquerque, NM 87102
(800) 472-8229
Fax (505) 243-8297
E-mail cookie@abq.com
Website www.janebutel.com

For flavored tortillas:
At this writing, one national brand, Mission, is making flavored tortillas.

INDEX

CONVERSION CHART

Equivalent Imperial and Metric Measurements

American cooks use standard containers, the 8-ounce cup and a Tablespoon that takes exactly 16 level fillings to fill that cup level. Measuring by cup makes it very difficult to give weight equivalents, as a cup of densely packed butter will weigh considerably more than a cup of flour. The easiest way therefore to deal with cup measurements in recipes is to take the amount by volume rather than by weight. Thus the equation reads: *1 cup = 240 ml = 8 fl. oz.*   *1/2 cup = 120 ml = 4 fl. oz.*

It is possible to buy a set of American cup measures in major stores around the world.

In the States, butter is often measured in sticks. One stick is the equivalent of 8 Tablespoons. One Tablespoon of butter is therefore the equivalent to 1/2 ounce/15 grams.

Solid Measures			
U.S. and Imperial Measures		*Metric Measures*	
ounces	*pounds*	*grams*	*kilos*
1		28	
2		56	
3 1/2		100	
4	1/4	112	
5		140	
6		168	
8	1/2	225	
9		250	1/4
12	3/4	340	
16	1	450	
18		500	1/2
20	1 1/4	560	
24	1 1/2	675	
27		750	3/4
28	1 3/4	780	
32	2	900	
36	2 1/4	1000	1
40	2 1/2	1100	
48	3	1350	
54		1500	1 1/2
64	4	1800	
72	4 1/2	2000	2
80	5	2250	2 1/4
90		2500	2 1/2
100	6	2800	2 3/4

Oven Temperature Equivalents			
Fahrenheit	Celsius	Gas Mark	Description
225	110	1/4	Cool
250	130	1/2	
275	140	1	Very Slow
300	150	2	
325	170	3	Slow
350	180	4	Moderate
375	190	5	
400	200	6	Moderately Hot
425	220	7	Fairly Hot
450	230	8	Hot
475	240	9	Very Hot
500	250	10	Extremely Hot

Liquid Measures			
Fluid ounces	*U.S.*	*Imperial*	*Milliliters*
	1 teaspoon	1 teaspoon	5
1/4	2 teaspoons	1 dessertspoon	10
1/2	1 Tablespoon	1 Tablespoon	14
1	2 Tablespoons	2 Tablespoons	28
2	1/4 cup	4 Tablespoons	56
4	1/2 cup		110
5		1/4 pint or 1 gill	140
6	3/4 cup		170
8	1 cup		225
9			250
10	1 1/4 cups	1/2 pint	280
12	1 1/2 cups		340
15		3/4 pint	420
16	2 cups		450
18	2 1/4 cups		500
20	2 1/2 cups	1 pint	560
24	3 cups		675
25		1 1/4 pints	700
27	3 1/2 cups		750
30	3 3/4 cups	1 1/2 pints	840
32	4 cups or 1 quart		900
35		1 3/4 pints	980
36	4 1/2 cups		1000
40	5 cups	2 pints or 1 quart	1120
48	6 cups		1350
50		2 1/2 pints	1400
60	7 1/2 cups	3 pints	1680
64	8 cups or 2 quarts		1800
72	9 cups		2000

EQUIVALENTS FOR INGREDIENTS

all-purpose flour—plain flour
arugula—rocket
powdered sugar—icing sugar
cornstarch—corn flour
eggplant—aubergine
granulated sugar—castor sugar
half and half—12% fat milk
lima beans—broad beans
scallion—spring onion
shortening—white fat
unbleached flour—strong, white flour
vanilla bean—vanilla pod
zest—rind
zucchini—courgettes or marrow